windmill

WITHDRAWN
rom Toronto Public Library

VGA
Enhanced 101 or 102 key US and Non US
Microsoft Mouse version 9.01
no Network installed

writing in Book
HP Apr. 29/03
281-3184

NUCLEAR ENERGY

NUCLEAR WASTE

EARTH • AT • RISK

Acid Rain

Alternative Sources of Energy

Animal Welfare

The Automobile and the Environment

Clean Air

Clean Water

Degradation of the Land

Economics of Environmental Protection

Environmental Action Groups

The Environment and the Law

Environmental Disasters

Extinction

The Fragile Earth

Global Warming

The Living Ocean

Nuclear Energy • Nuclear Waste

Overpopulation

The Ozone Layer

Recycling

The Rainforest

Solar Energy

Toxic Materials

What You Can Do for the Environment

Wilderness Preservation

EARTH • AT • RISK

NUCLEAR ENERGY

NUCLEAR WASTE

by Anne L. Galperin

Introduction by
Russell E. Train

Chairman of
the Board of Directors,
World Wildlife Fund and
The Conservation Foundation

CHELSEA HOUSE PUBLISHERS
new york   philadelphia

CHELSEA HOUSE PUBLISHERS
EDITOR-IN-CHIEF: Remmel Nunn
MANAGING EDITOR: Karyn Gullen Browne
COPY CHIEF: Mark Rifkin
PICTURE EDITOR: Adrian G. Allen
ART DIRECTOR: Maria Epes
ASSISTANT ART DIRECTOR: Noreen Romano
MANUFACTURING MANAGER: Gerald Levine
SYSTEMS MANAGER: Lindsey Ottman
PRODUCTION MANAGER: Joseph Romano
PRODUCTION COORDINATOR: Marie Claire Cebrián

EARTH AT RISK
Senior Editor: Jake Goldberg

Staff for *Nuclear Energy • Nuclear Waste*
ASSOCIATE EDITOR: Karen Hammonds
COPY EDITOR: Laurie Kahn
EDITORIAL ASSISTANT: Ian Wilker
PICTURE RESEARCHER: Villette Harris
DESIGNER: Maria Epes
LAYOUT: Marjorie Zaum

Copyright © 1992 by Chelsea House Publishers, a division of Main Line Book Co. All rights reserved. Printed and bound in the United States of America.

 This book is printed on recycled paper.

First printing

1 3 5 7 9 8 6 4 2

Library of Congress Cataloging-in-Publication Data
Galperin, Anne.
   Nuclear energy/nuclear waste/by Anne L. Galperin; introduction by Russell E. Train.
     p. cm.—(Earth at risk)
   Includes bibliographical references and index.
   Summary: Discusses nuclear power and how the positive benefits of nuclear energy are balanced against the problem of disposing of radioactive wastes.
   ISBN 0-7910-1585-8
      0-7910-1610-2 (paper)
   1. Nuclear energy—Juvenile literature. 2. Nuclear power plants—Juvenile literature. 3. Radioactive waste disposal—Juvenile literature. [1. Nuclear energy. 2. Nuclear power plants. 3. Radioactive waste disposal.] I. Title. II. Series.   91-15914
TK9148.G35 1991   CIP
333.792'4—dc20   AC

CONTENTS

Introduction—Russell E. Train   6

1 The Nuclear Age   13

2 The Atom and Radiation   25

3 The Nuclear Power Plant   39

4 Nuclear Waste   57

5 Nuclear Accidents   73

6 The Future of Nuclear Power   87

Appendix: For More Information   100

Further Reading   102

Glossary   104

Index   107

INTRODUCTION

Russell E. Train

Administrator, Environmental Protection Agency, 1973 to 1977; Chairman of the Board of Directors, World Wildlife Fund and The Conservation Foundation

There is a growing realization that human activities increasingly are threatening the health of the natural systems that make life possible on this planet. Humankind has the power to alter nature fundamentally, perhaps irreversibly.

This stark reality was dramatized in January 1989 when *Time* magazine named Earth the "Planet of the Year." In the same year, the Exxon *Valdez* disaster sparked public concern over the effects of human activity on vulnerable ecosystems when a thick blanket of crude oil coated the shores and wildlife of Prince William Sound in Alaska. And, no doubt, the 20th anniversary celebration of Earth Day in April 1990 renewed broad public interest in environmental issues still further. It is no accident then that many people are calling the years between 1990 and 2000 the "Decade of the Environment."

And this is not merely a case of media hype, for the 1990s will truly be a time when the people of the planet Earth learn the meaning of the phrase "everything is connected to everything else" in the natural and man-made systems that sustain our lives. This will be a period when more people will understand that burning a tree in Amazonia adversely affects the global atmosphere just as much as the exhaust from the cars that fill our streets and expressways.

Central to our understanding of environmental issues is the need to recognize the complexity of the problems we face and the relationships between environmental and other needs in our society. Global warming provides an instructive example. Controlling emissions of carbon dioxide, the principal greenhouse gas, will involve efforts to reduce the use of fossil fuels to generate electricity. Such a reduction will include energy conservation and the promotion of alternative energy sources, such as nuclear and solar power.

The automobile contributes significantly to the problem. We have the choice of switching to more energy efficient autos and, in the longer run, of choosing alternative automotive power systems and relying more on mass transit. This will require different patterns of land use and development, patterns that are less transportation and energy intensive.

In agriculture, rice paddies and cattle are major sources of greenhouse gases. Recent experiments suggest that universally used nitrogen fertilizers may inhibit the ability of natural soil organisms to take up methane, thus contributing tremendously to the atmospheric loading of that gas—one of the major culprits in the global warming scenario.

As one explores the various parameters of today's pressing environmental challenges, it is possible to identify some areas where we have made some progress. We have taken important steps to control gross pollution over the past two decades. What I find particularly encouraging is the growing environmental consciousness and activism by today's youth. In many communities across the country, young people are working together to take their environmental awareness out of the classroom and apply it to everyday problems. Successful recycling and tree-planting projects have been launched as a result of these budding environmentalists who have committed themselves to a cleaner environment. Citizen action, activated by youthful enthusiasm, was largely responsible for the fast-food industry's switch from rainforest to domestic beef, for pledges from important companies in the tuna industry to use fishing techniques that would not harm dolphins, and the recent announcement by the McDonald's Corporation to phase out polystyrene "clam shell" hamburger containers.

Despite these successes, much remains to be done if we are to make ours a truly healthy environment. Even a short list of persistent issues includes problems such as acid rain, ground-level ozone and smog, and airborne toxins; ground water protection and nonpoint sources of pollution such as runoff from farms and city streets; wetlands protection; hazardous waste dumps; and solid waste disposal, waste minimization, and recycling.

Similarly, there is an unfinished agenda in the natural resources area: effective implementation of newly adopted management plans for national forests; strengthening the wildlife refuge system; national park management, including addressing the growing pressure of development on lands surrounding the parks; implementation of the Endangered Species Act; wildlife trade problems, such as that involving elephant ivory; and ensuring adequate sustained funding for these efforts at all levels of government. All of these issues are before us today; most will continue in one form or another through the year 2000.

Each of these challenges to environmental quality and our health requires a response that recognizes the complex nature of the problem. Narrowly conceived solutions will not achieve lasting results. Often it seems that when we grab hold of one part of the environmental balloon, an unsightly and threatening bulge appears somewhere else.

The higher environmental issues arise on the national agenda, the more important it is that we are armed with the best possible knowledge of the economic costs of undertaking particular environmental programs and the costs associated with not undertaking them. Our society is not blessed with unlimited resources, and tough choices are going to have to be made. These should be informed choices.

All too often, environmental objectives are seen as at cross purposes with other considerations vital to our society. Thus, environmental protection is often viewed as being in conflict with economic growth, with energy needs, with agricultural productions, and so on. The time has come when environmental considerations must be fully integrated into every nation's priorities.

One area that merits full legislative attention is energy efficiency. The United States is one of the least energy efficient of all the industrialized nations. Japan, for example, uses far less energy per unit of gross national product than the United States does. Of course, a country as large as the United States requires large amounts of energy for transportation. However, there is still a substantial amount of excess energy used, and this excess constitutes waste. More fuel efficient autos and home heating systems would save millions of barrels of oil, or their equivalent, each year. And air pollutants, including greenhouse gases, could be significantly reduced by increased efficiency in industry.

I suspect that the environmental problem that comes closest to home for most of us is the problem of what to do with trash. All over the world, communities are wrestling with the problem of waste disposal. Landfill sites are rapidly filling to capacity. No one wants a trash and garbage dump near home. As William Ruckelshaus, former EPA administrator and now in the waste management business, puts it, "Everyone wants you to pick up the garbage and no one wants you to put it down!"

At the present time, solid waste programs emphasize the regulation of disposal, setting standards for landfills and so forth. In the decade ahead, we must shift our emphasis from regulating waste disposal to an overall reduction in its volume. We must look at the entire waste stream, including product design and packaging. We must avoid creating waste in the first place. To the greatest extent possible, we should then recycle any waste that is produced. I believe that, while most of us enjoy our comfortable way of life and have no desire to change things, we also know in our hearts that our "disposable society" has allowed us to become pretty soft.

Land use is another domestic issue that might well attract legislative attention by the year 2000. All across the United States, communities are grappling with the problem of growth. All too often, growth imposes high costs on the environment—the pollution of aquifers; the destruction of wetlands; the crowding of shorelines; the loss of wildlife habitat; and the loss of those special places, such as a historic structure or area, that give a community a sense of identity. It is worth noting that growth is not only the product of economic development but of population movement. By the year 2010, for example, experts predict that 75% of all Americans will live within 50 miles of a coast.

It is important to keep in mind that we are all made vulnerable by environmental problems that cross international borders. Of course, the most critical global conservation problems are the destruction of tropical forests and the consequent loss of their biological capital. Some scientists have calculated extinction rates as high as 11 species per hour. All agree that the loss of species has never been greater than at the present time; not even the disappearance of the dinosaurs can compare to today's rate of extinction.

In addition to species extinctions, the loss of tropical forests may represent as much as 20% of the total carbon dioxide loadings to the atmosphere. Clearly, any international approach to the problem of global warming must include major efforts to stop the destruction of forests and to manage those that remain on a renewable basis. Debt for nature swaps, which the World Wildlife Fund has pioneered in Costa Rica, Ecuador, Madagascar, and the Philippines, provide a useful mechanism for promoting such conservation objectives.

Global environmental issues inevitably will become the principal focus in international relations. But the single overriding issue facing the world community today is how to achieve a sustainable balance between growing human populations and the earth's natural systems. If you travel as frequently as I do in the developing countries of Latin America, Africa, and Asia, it is hard to escape the reality that expanding human populations are seriously weakening the earth's resource base. Rampant deforestation, eroding soils, spreading deserts, loss of biological diversity, the destruction of fisheries, and polluted and degraded urban environments threaten to spread environmental impoverishment, particularly in the tropics where human population growth is greatest.

It is important to recognize that environmental degradation and human poverty are closely linked. Impoverished people desperate for land on which to grow crops or graze cattle are destroying forests and overgrazing even more marginal land. These people become trapped in a vicious downward spiral. They have little choice but to continue to overexploit the weakened resources available to them. Continued abuse of these lands only diminishes their productivity. Throughout the developing world, alarming amounts of land rendered useless by overgrazing and poor agricultural practices have become virtual wastelands, yet human numbers continue to multiply in these areas.

From Bangladesh to Haiti, we are confronted with an increasing number of ecological basket cases. In the Philippines, a traditional focus of U.S. interest, environmental devastation is widespread as deforestation, soil erosion, and the destruction of coral reefs and fisheries combine with the highest population growth rate in Southeast Asia.

Controlling human population growth is the key factor in the environmental equation. World population is expected to at least double to about 11 billion before leveling off. Most of this growth will occur in the poorest nations of the developing world. I would hope that the United States will once again become a strong advocate of international efforts to promote family planning. Bringing human populations into a sustainable balance with their natural resource base must be a vital objective of U.S. foreign policy.

Foreign economic assistance, the program of the Agency for International Development (AID), can become a potentially powerful tool for arresting environmental deterioration in developing countries. People who profess to care about global environmental problems—the loss of biological diversity, the destruction of tropical forests, the greenhouse effect, the impoverishment of the marine environment, and so on—should be strong supporters of foreign aid planning and the principles of sustainable development urged by the World Commission on Environment and Development, the "Brundtland Commission."

If sustainability is to be the underlying element of overseas assistance programs, so too must it be a guiding principle in people's practices at home. Too often we think of sustainable development only in terms of the resources of other countries. We have much that we can and should be doing to promote long-term sustainability in our own resource management. The conflict over our own rainforests, the old growth forests of the Pacific Northwest, illustrates this point.

The decade ahead will be a time of great activity on the environmental front, both globally and domestically. I sincerely believe we will be tested as we have been only in times of war and during the Great Depression. We must set goals for the year 2000 that will challenge both the American people and the world community.

Despite the complexities ahead, I remain an optimist. I am confident that if we collectively commit ourselves to a clean, healthy environment we can surpass the achievements of the 1980s and meet the serious challenges that face us in the coming decades. I hope that today's students will recognize their significant role in and responsibility for bringing about change and will rise to the occasion to improve the quality of our global environment.

The well-known contours of a nuclear power plant cooling tower symbolize many things to many people, from technological accomplishment to imminent disaster.

chapter 1

THE NUCLEAR AGE

Along with food and shelter, energy has always been a basic human concern. Energy is the ability to do work—to plow fields, to transport people and things, to light and heat homes, to power machinery. There are still cultures in which people have only their own physical strength and that of domesticated animals to get work done and rely on fire for light, warmth, and cooking. Technologically advanced cultures have developed greater, more complex energy needs and a number of strategies to meet these needs. Humankind is faced with the challenge of satisfying its growing energy demands without jeopardizing human health and the environment.

There are many kinds of energy, including gravitational, thermal (heat), chemical, mechanical, and atomic. Atomic—or, more accurately, nuclear—energy is more powerful than any other kind. It is released by using the forces within the *nucleus*, or core, of an atom in one of two ways: through *fission*, which involves splitting the nucleus, or through *fusion*, the joining together of two nuclei. Both processes occur spontaneously in nature, but only fission can be controlled and used by humans to generate electricity. Scientists are trying to develop technology

The destruction wrought on Nagasaki, Japan, in 1945 by the U.S. nuclear bomb Fat Man testified to the fearsome power of nuclear energy.

that will enable them to harness the tremendous energy released by fusion as well.

In December 1942, in the middle of World War II, a team of scientists at the University of Chicago, led by the Italian-born physicist Enrico Fermi, demonstrated that they could produce nuclear fission by starting up and then controlling a nuclear *chain reaction*—a self-sustaining process in which the splitting of one atom triggers the splitting of other atoms, which in turn causes more fissions. Fermi's *atomic pile*—literally a pile of uranium fuel rods surrounded by graphite blocks—was the world's first nuclear reactor.

When carefully controlled, nuclear fission can be used to generate electrical power; uncontrolled fission can produce an enormous explosion. The nuclear age was formally ushered in during the final weeks of World War II, when the United States dropped nuclear bombs on the Japanese cities Hiroshima and Nagasaki. It became apparent to world governments, the international scientific community, and the general public that the amount of energy—and destruction—that could be unleashed by splitting the atom was formidable.

Nuclear weapons development—of both fission and thermonuclear, or fusion, bombs—continued after the war, but peaceful uses for this new technology developed as well. Growing energy needs prompted many nations to turn to nuclear fission as an abundant and seemingly inexpensive and safe source of electricity. In 1946, the U.S. Congress established the Atomic Energy Commission (AEC) to oversee the development of nuclear technology for peaceful as well as military purposes, and by 1951, the first nuclear power-generated electricity had been produced at an experimental reactor in Arco, Idaho.

In 1953, President Dwight D. Eisenhower presented the United Nations General Assembly with his "Atoms for Peace" plan, which portrayed nuclear energy as a big step in civilization's march forward and supported the exchange of information about nuclear technology among friendly nations. The first UN International Conference on the Peaceful Uses of Atomic Energy took place in 1955. Two years later, the International Atomic Energy Agency was established in Vienna, Austria, with a mandate from the UN to promote the "peaceful uses of atomic energy."

In the United States, the Atomic Energy Act of 1954 permitted private industry to develop and use nuclear energy, an activity that, for security reasons, had previously been restricted to government agencies. The AEC would license and oversee private industry in the construction and operation of nuclear power plants. In effect, government and industry became partners in developing and promoting this new energy source.

The first commercial nuclear power plant in the United States—a joint project of the AEC and the Duquesne Light Company—was powered up in 1957 in Shippingport, Pennsylvania, amid much fanfare. The promise of AEC chairman Lewis Strauss that plentiful nuclear electricity would be "too cheap to meter" seemed close at hand. Earlier that same year, however, the AEC had published a disturbing study entitled "Theoretical Possibilities and Consequences of Major Accidents in Large Nuclear Power Plants." The report concluded that a nuclear reactor accident could cause thousands of deaths and as much as $7 billion in property damage. This signaled to many that nuclear energy was not without hazards. To reassure the public and, in particular, the utilities involved in the nuclear power industry, Congress passed the Price-Anderson amendment to the Atomic Energy Act, which established a federal fund from which the victims of any nuclear plant accident would be compensated—although for only a fraction of the possible damage.

Several other nations developed nuclear power programs in the 1950s, including the Soviet Union, which built the first civilian-use reactor in 1954, and Great Britain, which was the first to develop a commercial nuclear power program. The industry continued to grow in the following decades as a number of other countries, including Canada, France, Sweden, Belgium, and Finland, began building reactors.

The 1970s signaled a turning point for nuclear power in the United States and many other countries. Although many reactors went *on-line*, or began operating, during the next two decades, the pace of development began to slow because of a combination of factors: rising costs, lower than anticipated demand for electricity (in part due to energy conservation efforts), and growing public fears over the safety of nuclear power.

NUCLEAR POWER TODAY

Close to one-fifth of the world's electricity is now generated by nuclear power plants. As of 1990, more than 400 plants were operating worldwide, in more than 30 countries. The amount of nuclear-generated electricity varies widely from country to country. Nuclear power provides France with almost 75% of its electricity, whereas the United States, which had 112

Physicist Enrico Fermi at the controls of an atom smasher. Fermi and his colleagues built the world's first full-scale nuclear reactor at the University of Chicago in 1942.

A Kiwi-A military reactor, used in experiments involving rocket propulsion in the late 1950s.

reactors licensed to operate in 1989, derives only about 20% of its electricity from this source—although that amount represents one-third of the electricity produced by nuclear power worldwide. The majority of electricity used in the United States—about 54% in 1989—is supplied by coal. Natural gas, oil, and hydroelectric power account for most of the remaining 26% of electricity sources.

Nuclear power is used to generate electricity at sea and in space as well as on land. Reactors can be used to power submarines, allowing them to remain underwater for longer periods of time without refueling, and ships, as well as satellites that orbit the earth for long periods. Some reactors are used to produce nuclear weapons materials rather than electrical power.

There are many other applications of nuclear technology besides electrical power generation and weapons production. Nuclear medicine uses radioactive chemicals—by-products of nuclear reactions—to diagnose and treat diseases such as cancer and hyperthyroidism. Nuclear materials are also used in various kinds of scientific research, such as the study of physiological processes of plants and animals.

Whereas the benefits of nuclear medicine are largely undisputed, those of nuclear power are much debated. Supporters of nuclear energy argue that it is a virtually unlimited source of electricity. Uranium is in fact a nonrenewable resource like fossil fuels. The earth's supplies of the mineral will last only a few hundred years—not much longer than coal, oil, and natural gas—unless special *breeder* reactors that produce as well as consume fissionable fuel are used, and serious problems continue to plague such reactors.

Proponents of nuclear power also assert that its use reduces U.S. dependence on foreign oil. Nuclear energy does not, with current technology, substantially reduce oil consumption: 6% at most of the oil used each year in the United States goes to generate electricity. It should also be noted that electricity—the only form of energy that nuclear power can practicably generate—represents only a fraction of total energy consumption. Automobiles and airplanes, for example, currently require gasoline fuel produced from crude oil. According to the U.S. Department of Energy, nuclear power provided only about 4% of the total energy consumed worldwide in 1987, whereas oil supplied 32%, coal 26%, natural gas 17%, and biomass (wood, dung, and crop residue) 15%.

It has also been argued that nuclear energy, unlike coal or oil, contributes little to pollution or to global warming, an apparent worldwide temperature increase caused by the buildup of carbon dioxide and other heat-trapping gases emitted by fossil fuels into the earth's atmosphere. This argument ignores two facts:

First, nuclear power harms the environment in different but equally damaging ways; second, coal-generated electrical power is needed to mine and process the uranium required to produce nuclear power. Moreover, as uranium ore supplies dwindle, more and more energy will have to be expended to obtain the mineral, increasing nuclear power's contribution to global warming.

Another key issue in the debate over nuclear power is that of safety. How safe is safe enough? Advocates and opponents of nuclear energy disagree on the level of risk that is actually involved and the amount of risk they themselves are willing to incur. Opponents, who cite the problem-filled history of nuclear power, are divided between those who are completely against its use and those who would consider supporting limited use if plants were better designed and managed.

No matter what type of reactor is used, generating nuclear energy always produces radioactive wastes and emissions. Used nuclear plant fuel is one such waste product. This *spent fuel*, as it is called, is highly radioactive and requires special storage and handling to prevent it from leaking into the environment. When nuclear power plants were first constructed, it seemed that the waste disposal problem would be easily solved by reprocessing and recycling spent fuel. But reprocessing has proved to be a high-risk activity in itself—one that generates plutonium, a highly radioactive element, and other radioactive waste materials. In addition, plutonium is a vital ingredient in nuclear bombs, and producing it in large quantities increases the risk of nuclear weapons proliferation. The hazards associated with fuel reprocessing have indefinitely delayed construction of reprocessing plants in the United States and created problems at plants elsewhere in the world; this problem, combined with the absence

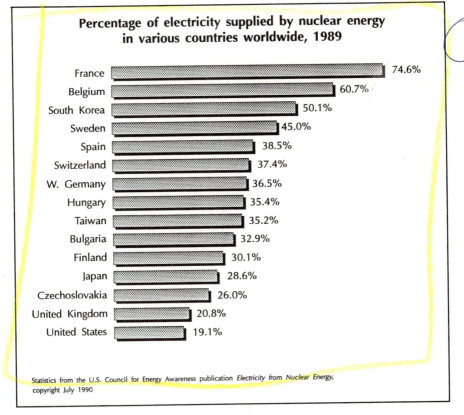

Statistics from the U.S. Council for Energy Awareness publication *Electricity from Nuclear Energy*, copyright July 1990

of long-term waste-storage facilities, has been a major setback for the nuclear power industry.

Several accidents have contributed to the climate of controversy surrounding nuclear power. A reactor accident in March 1979 at the Three Mile Island nuclear power plant near Harrisburg, Pennsylvania, demonstrated one serious danger inherent in nuclear power. In what was supposed to have been a highly unlikely accident, mechanical problems combined with human error resulted in a partial *meltdown*, or overheating of nuclear fuel, that forced the permanent shutdown of a reactor. Although there were no immediate fatalities and a total meltdown was averted, the accident contributed to mounting public questioning of the viability of nuclear power.

In addition to the accident at Three Mile Island, a 1986 disaster at the Chernobyl nuclear power station in the Soviet Union raised global awareness and concern about radiation and its effects. Radioactive pollution from Chernobyl resulted in at least 30 immediate deaths and approximately 1,000 cases of radiation sickness and has left the area virtually uninhabitable.

The safety record of military defense plants that produce nuclear materials for weapons has also come under scrutiny. In addition to reports citing unsafe working conditions and inadequate storage of radioactive waste, recent revelations of large releases of radioactive material into the environment at various military facilities, including the Hanford Nuclear Reservation in Washington State, have become a matter of widespread concern. In 1989, Secretary of Energy James D. Watkins criticized his own department for past problems and negligence at these plants. The U.S. government is planning a massive commitment of funds for cleanup efforts at its nuclear weapons facilities; costs may run higher than $200 billion over the next 60 years.

Expense is another problem that has plagued the nuclear power industry: Newer plants generate electricity for about twice the cost of coal-generated electricity, not including the costs of most waste disposal, accidents, research, and the *decommissioning*, or shutdown, of old plants. All of these expenses, whether paid for by utilities or the government, are ultimately passed on to consumers.

In part because of growing concerns about the safety of nuclear power and also because of growing costs, all orders in the

United States for nuclear power plants placed after 1974 were eventually canceled, although construction continued on many plants already begun. In recent years, public opposition has even prevented several already constructed plants from opening, including the Shoreham plant in New York and the Rancho Seco power station in California.

Internationally, nuclear power is thriving in some countries and faltering in others. Japan and the Soviet Union continue to invest in nuclear reactors, and South Korea and India are among the many nations developing nuclear capacity. In 1990, Czechoslovakia announced plans to double its number of reactors to 16, to the dismay of its nuclear-free neighbor Austria. At the same time, Sweden—at the request of its citizens—has begun to dismantle its working nuclear power plants, aiming to be nuclear free by the year 2010; there is also fierce public opposition to nuclear power in Germany. Austria and the Philippines both decided to scrap their only plants in the development stage because they were not cost-effective. Energy conservation and renewable sources of energy such as solar power are strategies being implemented throughout the world as alternatives to nuclear energy and fossil fuel use, with varying degrees of commitment and success.

How does nuclear power measure up? This question is being asked about every facet of nuclear power—from the mining and enrichment of uranium and other fuels to the design, construction, and operation of power plants to the handling and storage of radioactive nuclear wastes. A reasonable starting point in understanding the debate is a discussion of the atom itself, a tiny particle of matter that nevertheless has a mammoth potential.

Physicist J. Robert Oppenheimer (left) and General Leslie R. Groves inspect the base of the tower from which the nuclear test bomb Trinity was exploded in Alamogordo, New Mexico, in 1945.

chapter 2

THE ATOM AND RADIATION

Everything in the universe, including body cells, air, gold, pizza, bicycles, and water, is made of atoms. The word *atom* is taken from the Greek word *atomos,* meaning "indivisible." The concept dates back more than 2,000 years, to the time of the ancient Greek philosophers Leucippus and Democritus, who logically deduced that all matter was made up of invisibly small units, each having all the properties of the substances they composed and each impossible to break down further.

Scientific discoveries made during the first 3 decades of the 20th century proved that there is indeed an atom, a smallest characteristic component of the 92 natural and 16 man-made elements that compose all substances; in other words, it is the smallest unit that exhibits the properties of its particular element. But the ancient Greeks were wrong in believing that the atom was indivisible. Every atom—whether of silver or gold, oxygen or lead—comprises a variety of even smaller particles. The minute core of an atom, its nucleus, consists of closely packed particles called *protons,* which have a positive electric charge; negatively charged particles called *electrons* orbit the nucleus. This

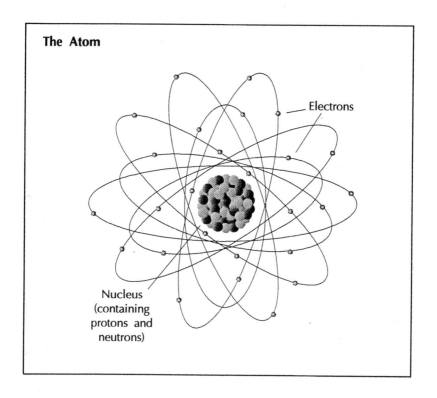

The Atom

Electrons

Nucleus (containing protons and neutrons)

explanation of atomic structure was developed by the early 20th century, in particular by the British physicist Ernest Rutherford.

Opposite electrical charges attract and like charges repel each other. The attraction between negatively charged electrons and positively charged protons holds the atom together. But within the nucleus, protons fiercely repel each other. These protons are held together by the so-called nuclear, or binding, force. If the protons are close enough to each other, as they are in simple atoms, the nuclear force binds them against the force of electric repulsion, and the atom is stable. *Neutrons*, electrically neutral particles within the nucleus, also exert this nuclear force and help bind the protons together. In elements such as uranium that have large nuclei containing many protons, even a great many neutrons cannot provide the binding force necessary to keep all the protons together; such atoms are said to be unstable. In their attempt to regain equilibrium, unstable nuclei shed pieces of themselves, releasing radiation in the form of a variety of destructive subatomic particles and *electromagnetic* waves, and sometimes spontaneously fission, each nucleus breaking into two smaller, nearly equal sized nuclei.

In the process of *radioactive decay*, the nucleus of an unstable atom continues to give off radiation until it reaches stability. In the course of decaying, the original atom may turn into a different *isotope*, an atom of the same element whose nucleus contains the same number of protons but a different number of neutrons. Uranium, for example, has 10 distinct isotopes, the most common of which is uranium-238, with 92 protons and 146 neutrons. Another, rarer isotope, uranium-235, contains 92 protons and 143 neutrons. The atom may also decay into another element altogether. For instance, uranium-238 decays into thorium and eventually to lead.

The length of time required for radioactive decay varies among different *radioisotopes* (isotopes that are unstable and emit destructive radiation) from a fraction of a second to millions of years. The duration of this process is measured according to a radioisotope's *half-life*—the time required for half of the atoms in a radioisotope sample to break down. The half-life of plutonium-239, for example, is 24,000 years; that of tritium, only 12.3 years.

The phenomenon of natural radioactivity was first observed by French physicist Antoine-Henri Becquerel in 1896 in the element uranium. Two years later, French scientists Pierre and Marie Curie discovered the naturally radioactive elements polonium and radium. The properties of radiation were also explored by German scientist Wilhelm Röntgen, who in 1896 found that bombarding certain matter with high-speed electrons produced a form of electromagnetic radiation, which he named the X ray. Rutherford, the first physicist to split atomic nuclei artificially, further contributed to radiation research. In the late 1920s, Frédéric and Irène Joliot-Curie (son-in-law and daughter of Marie and Pierre Curie) managed to create radioactive elements by bombarding stable isotopes with subatomic particles.

The next breakthrough following the Joliot-Curies' achievement was the discovery of the neutron by British physicist James Chadwick in 1932. Because neutrons carry no electrical charge, they are not deflected by other particles and so can easily penetrate a nucleus and destabilize it, or cause it to break apart. (If the neutron is absorbed but does not induce fission, a new, heavier isotope or element—such as plutonium—is created.)

Throughout the 1930s, scientists across Europe tried bombarding elements with neutrons to see what sort of nuclear reactions would occur. In Italy, Enrico Fermi found that more than 40 of the elements could be made radioactive, among them uranium, which behaved rather uniquely. When uranium was bombarded with neutrons, not only was radiation released, but a much smaller, lighter element was produced. The same result was achieved in Berlin by German scientists Otto Hahn and Fritz Strassmann. No one was sure what had happened, however, until 1939, when Austrian physicist Lise Meitner provided the answer: Fission had occurred, splitting the atom in half and producing radioactive barium. She also correctly deduced that the huge amount of energy released in the fission reaction confirmed Einstein's equation, $E = mc^2$ (where E = energy, m = mass, and c = the speed of light). A very small amount of matter can be converted into a huge amount of energy when the binding force holding the nucleus together is released during fission. It is the ability to break up heavy nuclei and convert their binding energy into heat that is the secret of nuclear power.

The products of uranium fission include the fragments of the split atom—mostly highly radioactive isotopes of elements such as iodine, cesium, and strontium—and two or three free neutrons. These free neutrons can cause other atoms to fission if a sufficient number of nuclei—called a *critical mass*—are available to capture the neutrons. Hungarian-born physicist Leo Szilard was the first to realize that sustained fission would release enormous amounts of energy, which, if uncontrolled, could be used as a bomb. With war impending in Europe, Szilard kept his theory to himself and quietly patented his ideas.

By the late 1930s, Szilard, Fermi, and many other scientists had left Europe for the United States. In 1939, in a laboratory at Columbia University in New York, Szilard and Fermi confirmed that uranium fission could release enough neutrons for a self-sustaining chain reaction. Although there was much more work to be done, their achievement suggested it might be possible to build a nuclear weapon. Many physicists who had recently arrived in the United States from Europe, where war was impending, supported the idea of developing a weapon to defeat Hitler's Germany. At Szilard's prompting, Albert Einstein wrote a letter to President Franklin D. Roosevelt urging him to finance the development of an atomic bomb. Roosevelt approved a secret military project code-named the Manhattan Project to develop, test, and build such a weapon. More than $2 billion was spent designing and building the huge laboratories and factories that sprang up all over the United States to test manufacturing techniques and to process nuclear materials. A new industry was created almost overnight.

Chain-reaction research was moved to the University of Chicago in 1942, where Fermi built the world's first full-scale nuclear reactor. There was a big difference, however, between Fermi's crude garage-sized reactor and a self-contained bomb that could be easily dropped from a plane. Hundreds of problems had to be solved, among them enriching the uranium so that a much smaller quantity of it could sustain a chain reaction.

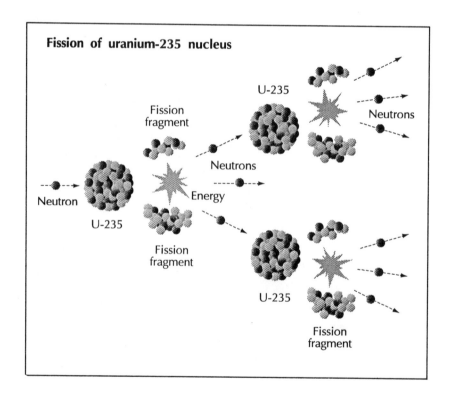

The final stage of designing and building the bomb took place at the Los Alamos Scientific Laboratory in New Mexico, in a project headed by Berkeley physicist J. Robert Oppenheimer. Oppenheimer recruited many talented physicists to Los Alamos, among them Edward Teller, who later developed the hydrogen, or thermonuclear, bomb, and Enrico Fermi. Ultimately, three bombs were built. The first, the project's plutonium test bomb, Trinity, was exploded in the New Mexico desert at dawn on July 16, 1945.

Isidor Isaac Rabi, a physicist who observed the Trinity test at Los Alamos, recalled, "Suddenly there was an enormous flash of light, the brightest light I have ever seen. . . . It blasted; it pounced; it bored its way right through you." The blast's extreme heat fused the desert sand into jade-green glass. The second bomb, Little Boy, was dropped on Hiroshima, Japan, on August 6, 1945. Its explosion was equivalent to that of 12,500 tons of TNT. Fat Man, the third bomb, was dropped on Nagasaki 3 days later and delivered a blast equal to 22,000 tons of TNT. The immediate death toll exceeded 200,000; thousands of people fatally injured by radiation died in the following weeks. The effects of these two bombs persist today. Some medical experts estimate that approximately 2,000 Japanese die each year from cancers caused by the explosions.

EFFECTS OF RADIATION

Destructive, or *ionizing*, radiation is invisible, tasteless, odorless, and inaudible. What, then, makes it so harmful? Exposure to radiation is bad for living things because it destroys the structure of atoms within body cells, the basic components of all living things. No matter where *radionuclides*, or atoms undergoing radioactive decay, happen to be located—in the body, in a glass of milk, or in the ocean—they affect other atoms around them. When they do not split and destroy atoms outright, their radiation tears electrons from atoms, turning the atoms into positively charged *ions* and changing their chemical and physical properties.

Radiation affects both germ cells and somatic cells. Germ cells are the reproductive cells—egg cells within a woman's ovaries, and sperm cells within a man's testes; all other body cells are somatic cells.

When germ cells are exposed to radiation, the genetic instructions they contain (in DNA, or deoxyribonucleic acid, molecules) can be damaged. Children conceived of damaged egg or sperm cells may suffer physical abnormalities, which will then be passed along to their offspring. Damage to genes ultimately damages the entire human species.

Radiation damage to an individual's somatic cells is confined to that person and cannot be passed on to offspring. Radiation can kill somatic cells or damage them so that they do not function normally. Sometimes these cells are able to repair themselves; sometimes not. The human body contains more cells than it needs, so a certain amount of cell damage can be tolerated. If damaged somatic cells live and reproduce, cancer or leukemia may ultimately result.

Radiation is particularly damaging to cells that grow and divide rapidly, such as those lining the digestive tract, cells in fetuses and children, the cells in bone marrow that mature into red blood cells, and reproductive cells. The parts of the body most sensitive to radiation are the thyroid, stomach, ovaries, testes, breasts, lungs, and bone marrow.

Radiation's ability to harm cells can also, fortunately, be harnessed to fight illnesses. In radiation therapy, radioactive chemicals are positioned within or on the body to destroy cancer cells, while healthy tissue is shielded. In a procedure known as "teletherapy," radiation from such isotopes as cobalt-60 can be aimed at a patient's cancerous tissue from a distance.

Ionizing radiation comes in several forms, including *alpha* and *beta* particles, neutrons, and electromagnetic waves. An alpha particle consists of two protons and two neutrons. This subatomic fragment is so large that it cannot pass through a piece of paper. Alpha particles travel only short distances. They are unable to penetrate skin, but radioactive substances that emit the particles can be swallowed, in contaminated food or water, or inhaled. The two protons create a powerful positive charge that makes the alpha particle an extremely destructive ionizer; it can easily strip electrons from atoms in body cells and break down or alter DNA molecules. One potent source of alpha radiation is radon gas, released in the process of uranium mining. Plutonium is also an alpha emitter.

Beta particles are high-speed electrons. They can penetrate an inch of flesh and cause serious burns and tissue damage. They can also be harmful when swallowed or inhaled but are not as damaging as alpha particles. Many nuclear waste products, including spent fuel, contain radioactive isotopes that emit beta radiation.

Because they have no electrical charge, neutrons can travel long distances through air and easily penetrate the body.

Neutrons are heavy compared to beta particles, and their momentum can break up large numbers of cells. Many nuclear power plant waste products are sources of neutrons.

Radiation is also emitted in the form of electromagnetic waves—rapid vibrations in electric and magnetic fields that consist of energy rather than mass. Gamma rays, emitted during radioactive decay, have the highest frequency and shortest wavelength and are the most destructive form of electromagnetic radiation. These rays easily penetrate the body and damage its cells.

Not all electromagnetic radiation is dangerous, however. Low-frequency, long-wavelength radio waves and ordinary light waves contain little destructive energy; higher frequency, shorter wavelength ultraviolet radiation and X rays are more damaging. Medical X rays have much less energy than gamma rays, although

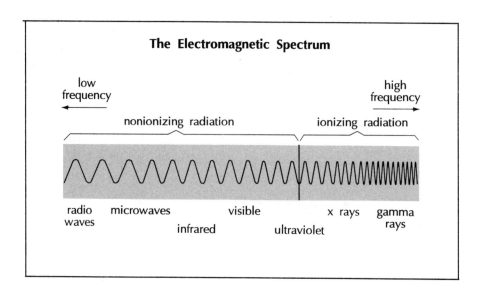

extensive exposure to them may result in the same physical disorders.

Units of measurement have been devised to describe the amount of radiation an individual has been exposed to; others describe the amount of damage to the body. These units are sometimes based upon a specific type of radiation. A *rad*, or radiation absorbed dose, describes the amount of ionizing radiation—regardless of type—deposited in body tissue. *Rem*, short for roentgen equivalent man, describes the biological impact of radiation. Some forms of radiation do more damage than others. One rem is roughly equal to the damage caused by 1 rad of gamma rays. One rad of alpha particles, however, causes 10 times the amount of damage caused by a gamma ray, or 10 rems' worth.

The average American is exposed to somewhere between 200 and 360 millirems of ionizing radiation yearly, depending on elevation and other factors. Approximately four-fifths of that total comes from naturally occurring elements and subatomic particles in the atmosphere and the earth and is called *background radiation*. Much of this is radon gas from decaying radioactive elements in the soil, building materials, and uranium mines. Radiation from the earth includes potassium in food and water and uranium and thorium in the ground. Other sources of background radiation are tritium and carbon-14 in the atmosphere. Bombardment by neutron radiation and other types of cosmic rays in the atmosphere is also common. The remaining exposure is man-made radiation, including fallout from nuclear weapons tests, nuclear plant wastes, medical X rays, nuclear medicine, and television and computer monitors.

The effects of radiation on the body vary, depending on the length, intensity, and area of exposure as well as the age and general health of the individual. Much of what is known about the effects of acute whole-body radiation exposure comes from the aftermath of the Hiroshima and Nagasaki bombings. A dose of 3,000 rads or more causes extreme damage to the brain and central nervous system. Death follows within hours. Four hundred to 3,000 rads causes death within a few weeks, as the severely damaged digestive system disintegrates and hemorrhages and infections set in. Two hundred fifty rads is considered the 50% lethal dose—within 2 months, half of those exposed will die of damage to blood vessels and bone marrow. One hundred rads will burn the skin. As little as 5 rads can cause vomiting and diarrhea.

There is much controversy over the long-term effects of low-level radiation. Some medical experts believe that there is a certain threshold level of radiation below which human health is not endangered; others feel there is no safe level of radiation exposure. Over long periods of time, even low-level radiation may lead to an increased risk of cancer and birth defects, higher infant and geriatric mortality rates, and lowered resistance to disease. Evaluating the hazards of low-level radiation is difficult because it often takes 30 to 40 years for the effects of small doses of radiation to become apparent; studies performed on populations with more recent exposures may not show anything unusual. Furthermore, radiation exposure results not in new diseases but in disorders such as cancer that are already prevalent in the general population. The actual source of the illness can therefore be difficult to determine.

Several organizations periodically report on the health effects of radiation, including the National Research Council's Committee on the Biological Effects of Ionizing Radiation and the United Nations Scientific Committee on the Effects of Atomic Radiation. Recent studies suggest that radiation is much more damaging than current safety regulations allow for. As the dangers of radiation become clearer, the nuclear power industry faces increasing pressure to operate plants and dispose of nuclear waste more safely.

A technician inspects uranium fuel assemblies, approximately 16,000 of which will be loaded into a reactor at the Hanford Reservation in Washington State.

chapter 3

THE NUCLEAR POWER PLANT

Power plants produce electricity by using some form of energy, such as fossil fuels or nuclear fission, to boil water into steam. Steam turns a turbine—a shaft with vanes at one end and a rotating magnet surrounded by a wire coil at the other. When the magnet rotates it produces an electric current in the coil. Current is transmitted by wires into homes and office buildings, where it powers appliances and machines. The generation of electricity from nuclear power is often described in terms of the *nuclear fuel cycle*, which begins with the mining of uranium for fuel and ends many steps later with the disposal and decay of power plant waste materials.

THE FRONT END OF THE FUEL CYCLE

Nuclear power demands a steady supply of uranium fuel. *Front end* processes are those that prepare uranium ore for reactor use. First, uranium ore is mined from the earth. (In the United States, most uranium mining occurs in the western states of Colorado, Utah, Wyoming, and New Mexico; other countries that mine the ore include France, Australia, the Soviet Union, and South Africa.) Next, the uranium ore is ground up and chemically treated to extract as much uranium as possible, which is made into a solid product called "yellowcake."

Almost all natural uranium atoms occur in the form of the stable isotope uranium-238. Less than 1% of natural uranium is the highly fissionable isotope uranium-235. For reactor use, uranium must usually be *enriched* so that the percentage of fissionable uranium-235 is increased to between 3% and 4%. To do this, yellowcake must be converted into a gaseous form, uranium hexafluoride, or UF_6, on which enrichment can be performed. In the United States, this process is done in government-owned enrichment plants.

In the enrichment process UF_6 gas is pushed through several screens. Because uranium-235 atoms are lighter than atoms of uranium-238, they move through first and are captured. This process is repeated several hundred times until the gas on the other side of the screen contains a high concentration of uranium-235. Many tons of natural uranium must be mined and processed to obtain just one ton of enriched uranium.

The enriched UF_6 is then returned to a solid form, uranium dioxide, and shaped into two-thirds-inch-long pellets, each encased in a ceramic shell. These are packed into 12-foot-long thin zirconium alloy fuel rods, grouped by hundreds and welded into fuel assemblies, which are then shipped to reactors for use.

Uranium enrichment converters at the Paducah Gaseous Diffusion Plant in Kentucky. Most nuclear reactors require fuel that has been processed to increase its percentage of fissionable uranium.

REACTOR OPERATION

The basic parts of a typical nuclear power plant include the reactor, where uranium fuel undergoes fission; steam-carrying tubes and heat-transfer systems; the turbine and generator; the control room, with its sensors and computers; the cooling systems; hundreds of valves; and miles of electrical, air, and water lines. Nuclear power plants are generally built close to rivers, lakes, and oceans, which provide a ready source of water for cooling.

The heart of a nuclear power plant is its reactor core, which typically contains a few hundred fuel assemblies. The reactor core is encased in a pressure vessel, a steel tank with walls several inches thick. In most reactors this vessel is enclosed in a containment structure, a steel-reinforced concrete dome that is generally three feet thick and serves as the outermost barrier between the plant and the environment, preventing most radiation from escaping the plant.

To start a reaction, nuclear fuel is bombarded with neutrons. Uranium atoms in the fuel absorb these neutrons, become more unstable, and then fission. This reaction releases heat, along with more neutrons and any of more than 80 radioactive fission products—such as strontium-90, cesium-137, and iodine-131—in solid or gaseous form. In the chain reaction described in Chapter 2, newly released neutrons hit other uranium atoms and cause them to fission, perpetuating the process. When the number of neutrons absorbed by the uranium atoms equals the number of neutrons created by fission, a reactor is said to be *self-sustaining*, or no longer reliant on the addition of neutrons from the outside. The amount of energy and radiation released increases with the number of neutrons released and the rate at which they are absorbed by uranium atoms.

The nuclear chain reaction is controlled with neutron-absorbing rods of cadmium or boron. Interlaced with fuel rods within the fuel assemblies, these control rods can speed up, slow down, or shut down the fission process altogether. The nuclear reaction's speed depends on the number of control rods inserted into the fuel and the extent of their insertion. With the control rods out, the nuclear reaction proceeds at its own pace, which is excessive for power production and leads to overheating and meltdown. When control rods are completely inserted into the reactor core, no new reactions occur, although those already begun run their course. In an emergency, automatic or manual systems might completely insert all the control rods; this procedure is called a *scram.*

Nuclear fission produces a tremendous amount of heat. The temperature within a *light-water* reactor (the most common type of reactor) typically reaches 600 degrees Fahrenheit (315 degrees Celsius), while inside the fuel rods it may reach 4000°F (2204°C). Coolant keeps the core's temperature under control and moves heat energy to an exchanger or directly to a turbine. Water is the most common coolant; it may be used as is or in a "heavy" form. Whereas ordinary "light" water contains hydrogen atoms with no neutrons, the hydrogen isotopes in heavy-water molecules—deuterium and tritium—contain one and two neutrons, respectively. The additional neutrons increase heavy water's density, making it a more effective coolant. Boric acid can be added to cooling water to absorb additional neutrons and help keep the reactor under control. Other reactor coolants include air, carbon dioxide, and helium and sodium gases. Nuclear plants are also built with an *emergency core-cooling system* designed to flood the reactor core should normal cooling procedures fail, although even this backup system is not necessarily foolproof.

In many reactors the coolant material is also used as a moderator. When neutrons pass through the moderator substance in the reactor core, they move against the molecules of the moderator and are slowed down, enabling them to penetrate uranium nuclei more easily. The density of heavy water makes it an especially good moderator, one that permits the reactor to run on unenriched fuel. Other moderators include graphite and beryllium.

TYPES OF REACTORS

All commercial nuclear power plants in the United States and more than three-quarters of those worldwide are light-water reactors, of two types: *boiling-water* reactors and *pressurized-water* reactors. Both types use ordinary water as coolant and moderator and require enriched uranium fuel. U.S. companies that manufacture these reactors include the General Electric Company, Westinghouse Electric Corporation, the Babcock & Wilcox Company, and Combustion Engineering.

Fuel assemblies in boiling-water reactors are surrounded by cooling water. The heat of nuclear fission makes the water boil; the steam produced is carried away from the core to the turbines. Once its work is done, the steam is condensed to water and returned to the reactor. The radiation released by fission contaminates the water and steam within the reactor core. One drawback to boiling-water reactors is that the turbine has direct contact with the radioactive steam. The entire system of core, steam and water lines, turbine, and condenser must be housed within a pressure vessel to prevent radioactive particles and gases from escaping. Even with this precaution, some radiation leaks into the surrounding air and water, which must periodically be filtered before being released outside the plant.

The more commonly used pressurized-water reactor helps solve the radioactive contamination problem by sealing the cooling water in a closed loop and adding a heat-exchange system. Water in the reactor core is kept under high pressure so that although it gets very hot, it does not become steam. The hot water is piped through a steam generator, where it converts a secondary water supply into steam to power the turbine. Unlike a boiling-water reactor, the pressure vessel contains only the reactor core and the primary water loop. The two water supplies do not mix unless a pipe leaks or ruptures, events that do sometimes occur.

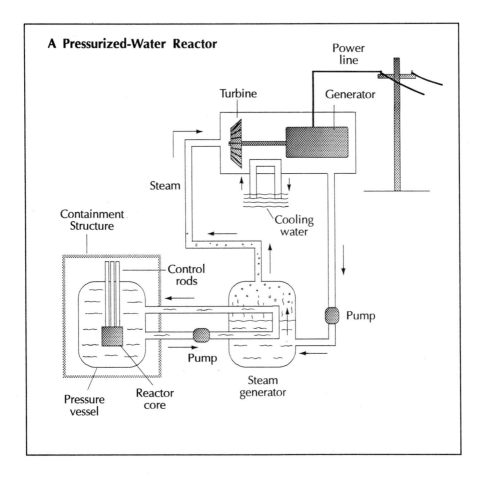

A version of the pressurized-water reactor called the CANDU (Canadian Deuterium Uranium reactor) is used for commercial power production in Canada. Uranium fuel is placed inside hundreds of pressure tubes through which coolant is pumped. The CANDU reactors use heavy water as both coolant and moderator, which permits them to run at lower pressure and on unenriched uranium. The primary water loop converts ordinary water in a separate circuit to steam for the turbine.

Gas-cooled reactors are similar to pressurized-water reactors except that helium or carbon dioxide gas replaces water in the primary loop. Some gas-cooled reactors use unenriched uranium, whereas others require enriched fuel. Solid graphite is used as a moderator. Gas-cooled reactors cost more to construct and operate than light-water reactors but are more energy-efficient because they operate at a higher temperature. The French and British use this type of reactor for commercial power production.

Breeder reactors are significantly different from other types because they produce more fissionable material than they consume. Breeders are fueled with a combination of plutonium and uranium. Plutonium fission releases neutrons that change nonfissionable uranium-238 into fissionable plutonium-239, which can be harvested from the reactor, reprocessed, and reused. Breeder reactors are economically viable for energy production where uranium resources are scarce; their use would theoretically extend uranium supplies by 50 times. However, it is estimated to take between 10 and 60 years for a breeder reactor to generate enough plutonium fuel to replace its fuel core.

Another drawback to breeders is their riskiness, in terms of both public health and national security. Plutonium is one of the most toxic and radioactive substances on earth; one atom inhaled and lodged within an individual's lungs leads inevitably to lung cancer. It is impossible to keep 100% of the plutonium used and produced by breeders isolated and away from direct human contact. According to medical physicist John Gofman, "Plutonium is so hazardous, that if you had a fully developed nuclear economy with breeder reactors fueled with plutonium, and you managed to contain the plutonium 99.99% perfectly, it would still cause somewhere between 140,000 and 500,000 extra lung cancer fatalities each year." Plutonium is also a necessary component of nuclear bombs and other weapons. Many nations use breeders to produce plutonium for this purpose. Their commercial use increases the risk of plutonium theft.

Another dangerous aspect of breeder reactors is that their coolant, liquid sodium, is a volatile element that explodes when exposed to water. A break in a sodium line can cause a blast powerful enough to break open the containment structure and spew radioactive particles and gases from the plant. Liquid sodium is also highly flammable when exposed to air, and leaks of the coolant frequently cause fires.

Because of these risks, a U.S. government project to build and test a breeder reactor in Tennessee has been delayed indefinitely. In France, the Superphénix breeder reactor, powered up in 1986, was shut down the following year because of sodium coolant leakage and may never reopen because of the cost of repairs. Other countries may delay or cancel plans to build commercial breeders in response to the French plant's difficulties and because of the current lack of demand for electricity.

THE BACK END OF THE FUEL CYCLE

The *back end* of the fuel cycle refers to the removal, reprocessing, and storage of spent fuel and other wastes (see Chapter 4 for details on waste storage). Individual uranium atoms in fuel rods can fission only once; eventually, the fuel becomes less able to sustain chain reactions. When reactor fuel is depleted, it must be removed and replaced. In boiling-water and pressurized-water reactors, fuel rods have a life expectancy of three to four years. Routine plant maintenance includes shutting down the reactor, removing old fuel assemblies, and replacing them with fresh fuel. Each year, one-third to one-fourth of the fuel rods are removed and replaced. These rods consist mostly of uranium, as well as a small percentage of plutonium and other fission products. This spent fuel is extremely radioactive and presents a serious disposal problem.

In the early years of the nuclear power industry, it was believed that spent fuel could be reprocessed so that its uranium content would be reenriched and reused and its plutonium extracted; the remaining waste would be both smaller in volume and dangerously radioactive for a much shorter time period— 10,000 rather than 240,000 years. Reprocessing sounds deceptively simple: Used fuel rods are dissolved in toxic acids, and the plutonium and uranium are extracted. The remaining waste and fission products still contain high levels of radioactivity, however, and require careful disposal. Plants must be carefully designed to shield workers and the environment from radiation. Much of the work must be performed by remote control, although equipment repairs and cleanup often need to be

Technicians assemble fuel pellets at a processing plant in Los Alamos, New Mexico. Extreme precautions must be taken to shield workers handling highly radioactive materials.

done manually by workers wearing protective clothing. Reprocessing-plant emissions are also dangerous, containing radioisotopes of plutonium, iodine, krypton, tritium, and carbon. Controlling these emissions may be beyond the ability of the nuclear industry, both economically and technologically. Reprocessing also requires extreme security measures to prevent the theft of weapons-grade plutonium.

The only venture into commercial reprocessing in the United States to date was Nuclear Fuel Services in West Valley, New York, which operated between 1966 and 1971. Critics charged that radioactive releases into the environment and overexposure of workers to radiation were routine. Nuclear Fuel Services was closed, ostensibly for expansion. Five years later, the plant was deemed uneconomical and permanently shut down.

In 1977, U.S. president Jimmy Carter delayed plans for commercial reprocessing because of the many hazards involved. In 1981, President Ronald Reagan lifted the unofficial ban, but the risk and costliness of the procedure appear to have prevented industry development to date. The few reprocessing plants abroad have been plagued with problems, including an explosion in 1973 at the Windscale plant in England that released radioactive gases and severely contaminated workers. In 1976, workers went on strike at the Cap de la Hague reprocessing plant in France over unsafe working conditions. U.S. government plans for permanent spent-fuel storage indicate that a high-level waste repository, not reprocessing, is favored for the future. Without reprocessing, it should be noted, the nuclear fuel cycle is open-ended, rendering the term *cycle* somewhat inaccurate.

DECOMMISSIONING

The maximum operating life of a nuclear power plant allowed by U.S. law is 40 years. Over time, continual neutron bombardment of the reactor vessel causes it to become brittle and more prone to rupture if the fuel overheats. Also, radiation that escapes the core gradually contaminates surrounding materials, from pipes to the containment structure itself, eventually rendering the plant unusable. Decommissioning refers to the cleanup that takes place when a plant is put out of service.

Once spent fuel is removed from a reactor, any of several decommissioning options can be selected. The plant can be *mothballed*, in which limited decontamination is carried out and the plant is closed and kept under guard (if desired, it can be reopened). When a plant is put into *entombment*, its radioactive components are sealed off with concrete and steel barriers. Total *dismantlement* involves the removal and disposal of all radioactive materials; the plant may first be mothballed for several decades to reduce its radioactivity. Another option is to convert a nuclear power plant to run on another type of fuel, such as coal or natural gas.

Estimates for decommissioning costs range widely, from as little as $170 million—a figure dismissed as too low by most industry analysts—to as much as $3 billion for a large reactor. To put these figures into context, it costs $4 billion to $9 billion over 15 years to build a plant that will *optimally* provide $12 billion worth of electricity—if it operates at full capacity for its projected 40-year life span. In reality, U.S. plants operate at only about 60% of capacity and do not last more than 30 years. A fully operational U.S. plant has yet to be completely decommissioned, although many reactors are coming to the end of their working lives—in most cases sooner than expected.

REGULATION AND REACTOR SAFETY

Commercial nuclear power plants in the United States are generally owned and operated by electrical utility companies and regulated by the Nuclear Regulatory Commission. In Canada, the industry is overseen by the Atomic Energy Control Board. Other countries have similar regulatory agencies.

Originally, the Atomic Energy Commission both regulated and promoted the commercial nuclear power industry in the United States. This conflict of interest ended in 1974, when the organization was divided into two branches. The NRC inherited the AEC's regulatory functions, while nuclear promotion and research became the province of the Energy Research and Development Administration, whose responsibilities were absorbed by the Department of Energy in 1977.

The NRC licenses and inspects nuclear power plants in the design and construction stages and throughout their operation. The agency investigates allegations of unsafe operation, accidents, and unusual occurrences. Corrections may be ordered, utilities may be fined, and operating licenses may be suspended or revoked. The NRC also regulates uranium mining and enrichment facilities and works jointly with the U.S. Department of Transportation to oversee shipments of radioactive materials.

Forty years ago, the U.S. government sought to encourage private industry's participation in commercial nuclear power. Presenting industry with too many expensive rules and regulations, it was feared, could have jeopardized the venture. The conflict between the need for safer plants and the desire to perpetuate the nuclear power industry—now a multi-billion-dollar business—continues today, in the wake of numerous reactor accidents and near misses. Utilities and manufacturers still complain that the NRC overregulates them, whereas those concerned with plant safety think the NRC does not do enough.

Nuclear power plants are potentially dangerous environments. Great caution must be exercised to prevent radiation contamination both within and outside the plant and to prevent reactor accidents from occurring. Nuclear plants also share certain hazards with other types of electricity-generating plants, including high-voltage electricity and high-pressure steam lines.

Reactors are run from a central control room. Although some procedures are performed manually, operators are assisted by sensors that monitor a variety of conditions inside the reactor, including pressure, water levels, and temperature. Should there be a malfunction, automatic systems connected to the sensors can make adjustments or shut down the reactor. Reactor operators can then take over or override safety systems altogether. Both options pose a significant chance of human error. The majority of U.S. nuclear power plant accidents are in fact caused by operator error, although mechanical malfunctions are sometimes a contributing factor.

The quality of operator training in the United States is often questioned. Utility companies are responsible for training their employees, who must then pass NRC-administered exams. Critics complain that operators are taught not to understand how a reactor works but rather to respond by rote to a specified set of circumstances. As a result, it is argued, they are ill prepared to deal with the unexpected scenarios that sometimes occur. That no two reactor units are exactly alike also hampers the development of adequate, comprehensive training programs: An operator at one Three Mile Island reactor, for example, would be unable to operate another unit at the same—or any other—plant.

Are nuclear power plants designed, constructed, and operated safely enough? Accident statistics compiled in recent years by the NRC itself are not very reassuring. According to statistics obtained from the NRC by Public Citizen, a public-interest advocacy group, more than 34,300 mishaps of various

Nuclear power plants are run from a central control room, where operators are assisted by various sensors and computers.

kinds occurred in the United States in the 1980s. The following problems were reported for 1987 alone.

- A total of 2,940 mishaps occurred at U.S. power plants, including some serious accidents.
- At least 430 scrams took place.
- There were approximately 104,000 incidents of worker exposure to measurable amounts of radiation.
- At least 492 violations of safety regulations took place, with the NRC issuing 45 fines totaling $2,740,833.

As orders for new plants have trailed off in the United States, the NRC has shifted its focus from licensing to monitoring existing plants more carefully. The agency has a formidable task, however. Although many new safety features are being implemented nationwide, the current generation of plants is aging, and as plants age and their components wear out, they become increasingly prone to mechanical failures and accidents.

RADIATION STANDARDS

No matter how safely a plant is run, low-level radioactive material is periodically released through vents and cooling water during routine operation. Whereas the Environmental Protection Agency (EPA) sets the nation's overall environmental radiation standards, the NRC oversees radiation releases generated by the nuclear power industry and sets limits on worker exposure within plants and on releases outside the plants. From the design stage onward, plants must prove that they are operating within these boundaries.

Nuclear plant radiation exposures and releases are guided by a general principle known as ALARA, which stands for As Low As Reasonably Achievable. Plants are informally limited to no more than 5 curies of radioactivity in vented liquids and gases each year. (A curie is a measure of radiation activity equal to 37 billion nuclear disintegrations per second.) Individuals outside the plant may be exposed to a maximum of 3 millirems of liquid-borne and 5 millirems of airborne radioactivity annually.

The NRC radiation exposure limits for power plant workers vary by the area of exposure and workers' age. Whole body exposure is limited to 5 rems per year. Individuals who work near the core handling radioactive materials wear protective clothing and radiation-measuring devices. The yearly radiation exposure limit for nuclear power plant workers is 50 times that for the general public.

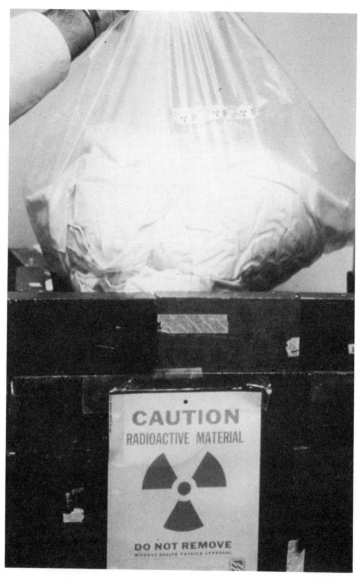
Nuclear industries generate a huge quantity and variety of radioactive materials, including medical waste.

chapter 4

NUCLEAR WASTE

Radioactive wastes come in many different forms, including the protective clothing of nuclear plant employees and other workers in contact with radioactive materials; the remains of lab animals used in experiments with radionuclides; cooling water, used fuel rods, and old tools and parts from nuclear power plants; *mill tailings* from uranium-enrichment factories; old medical radiation equipment from hospitals and clinics; and even used smoke detectors, which contain radioactive americium-241 sensors.

The creation of huge quantities of long-lived radioactive waste is the most formidable problem facing the nuclear power industry today. The difficulty of waste disposal was not considered a serious deterrent to commercial power production when plants were first promoted. It was assumed that waste could be reprocessed or buried somehow, or that another solution would be found. Unfortunately, finding safe ways of storing radioactive wastes so that they do not leak radiation into the environment has proved more difficult than anticipated.

THE SPREAD OF RADIATION

The planet's *hydrological*, or water, cycle is the main vehicle for conveying radiation through the environment. Lakes, streams, rivers, and oceans are visible sources of the earth's water; it is also contained within the earth as groundwater. The topmost layer of groundwater is known as the water table. The water table is closer to the earth's surface during rainy seasons and in regions with wet climates. The ground above the water table is relatively dry, the ground below it very moist. Underground water eventually joins lakes, streams, rivers, and oceans. Surface water and that released by plants evaporates into the air and turns into water vapor, which condenses to form clouds. Clouds release precipitation in the form of rain or snow, which falls into bodies of water or is absorbed by the earth.

When radioactive waste mixes with water it is ferried through this water cycle. Radionuclides in water are absorbed by surrounding vegetation and ingested by local marine and animal life. Radiation can also be airborne, deposited on people, plants, animals, and soil. Human beings can inhale or ingest radionuclides in air, drinking water, and food. The effects of leakage from poorly contained radioactive waste depend on how quickly that waste dissolves into the water supply, how rapidly it travels through the environment, and the half-life of individual radionuclides and how long they remain inside the human body.

According to a report on nuclear waste released by the U.S. National Academy of Sciences in 1983, it will take *3 million years* for radioactive waste stored in the United States as of that year to decay to background levels. Isolating this waste from the environment for even a fraction of that time period is a

Radioactive waste is unloaded at an underground storage facility in New Mexico.

mind-boggling prospect. As the September 1976 Flowers Report to the British Parliament concluded, "In considering arrangements for dealing safely with such wastes man is faced with time scales that transcend his experience." Radioactive waste disposal poses political as well as technological problems: No one wants it stored near *them*. This fear is understandable, yet a dire need for safe disposal exists, and repositories must be built somewhere. In the United States, developing and overseeing waste-storage facilities is the responsibility of the Department of Energy.

HIGH-LEVEL WASTE

Nuclear waste is divided into several categories. *High-level* waste consists mostly of spent nuclear reactor fuel from both commercial power plants and military facilities, as well as reprocessed materials and *transuranic* elements—those that are heavier than natural isotopes of uranium, such as plutonium. High-level waste can emit large amounts of radiation for hundreds of thousands of years. Commercial nuclear power plants in the United States alone produce 3,000 tons of high-level waste each year. The amount of spent fuel removed annually from 100 reactors would fill a football field to a depth of 1 foot.

When spent fuel is removed from a reactor core, it still emits millions of rems of radiation. A spent fuel rod contains 94% irradiated uranium. A variety of plutonium isotopes make up 1% of the spent fuel; other fission products constitute the remainder.

In the absence of high-level waste repositories, nuclear power plants generally store their spent fuel rods on-site in lead-lined concrete pools of water. These pools keep the rods relatively cool and somewhat contain the spread of gamma radiation. Metal grids in the pool maintain space between the cores, and boron in the metal grids helps absorb neutrons and prevent fission. The average commercial power plant puts 60 used assemblies into temporary storage each year and will probably continue to do so until the year 2000, when responsibility for spent fuel will be transferred to the Department of Energy. On-site storage is intended to be a temporary measure, and space is running out at many plants.

Temporary storage options for spent fuel include off-site storage pools. These would have to be built in earthquake-free areas near a source of water for coolant. Another alternative sometimes permitted by the NRC is for plants to store their spent fuel at other plants still under construction. It is theoretically possible to reduce the amount of storage space that spent fuel rods require by removing them from their assemblies, bundling them tightly, and then packing them into heavily shielded dry storage. But repacking these highly radioactive rods may present too much of a challenge to ever become a reality.

PERMANENT REPOSITORIES

Long-term storage of high-level waste requires a waterproof, geologically stable repository and leak-proof waste containers. Packaging has to be tailored to the volume of the waste, the isotopes it contains, how radioactive it is, its isotopes' half-lives, and how much heat it still generates.

One technique for packaging high-level wastes involves melting them with glass and pouring the molten material into impermeable containers. The containers could be buried in soil or in a rock pile and surrounded by fill material and a barrier wall. In 1990, the Department of Energy began test operations at a new radioactive waste–processing plant in South Carolina. The plan is to encase radioactive material in strong glass logs wrapped in steel. Two other plants may also be built, one in New York and another in Washington State. Another technique for treating high-level wastes is being tested at the Oak Ridge National Laboratory in Tennessee, where scientists are using microwaves to concentrate and solidify waste for safer disposal.

From the 1940s through the 1960s, barrels of radioactive waste were frequently dumped in oceans. The practice ended in 1970; 10 years later, the EPA determined that at least one-fourth of these barrels were leaking. New, possibly safer proposals under consideration for long-term ocean storage include offshore drilling and a procedure known as self-burial. In the first option, holes would be drilled into the seabed and filled with barrels of waste; in the second, specially shaped barrels would be dumped and left to sink to the ocean floor.

Geologic disposal is currently the most popular solution for waste disposal and one in which the U.S. government invested more than $2 billion during the 1980s. In this form of disposal, a mined cavity of tunnels with deep holes for waste canisters would be built using conventional mining techniques. Monitoring and waste retrieval would be relatively easy. Natural rock salt formations are the favored geologic medium for waste disposal because the presence of salt suggests the absence of water, which can corrode storage containers and conduct radiation throughout the ecosystem. Granite, hardened volcanic ash, basalt, clay, and shale are other geologic formations that may be suitable for radioactive waste disposal.

The 1982 Nuclear Waste Policy Act launched plans for the first permanent high-level commercial nuclear waste storage repository in the United States. Responsibilities for site selection, building, and operation were given to the Department of Energy. In 1987, a site was chosen: Yucca Mountain, 100 miles northwest of Las Vegas, Nevada. Expected to cost up to $15 billion, the repository at Yucca Mountain is scheduled to go into operation by the year 2010. Controversy is brewing, however, over the potential hazards posed by groundwater beneath the mountain. Although most experts involved in the project believe the site—a volcanic rock formation—is dry and that groundwater poses no risk, some project geologists, notably Jerry S. Szymanski, disagree. Based on the existence of extensive mineral deposits that he believes were caused by groundwater pushed up through the rock by earthquakes, Szymanski is convinced that the site is unsuitable. He envisions the possibility of groundwater flooding the dump and vaporizing among the hot canisters, rupturing them and releasing radiation. Szymanski's findings led the state of Nevada to file a lawsuit against the Department of Energy, temporarily halting most on-site testing.

Another U.S. government waste-disposal experiment is a project planned to test the viability of burial in rock salt formations. In 1990, the DOE received preliminary clearance from the Environmental Protection Agency to bury several thousand barrels of radioactive waste from nuclear weapons plants in salt beds near Carlsbad, New Mexico. Once in place,

A cutaway view of a proposed high-level waste repository in Lyons, Kansas. Safety concerns caused the plan to be shelved in the 1970s.

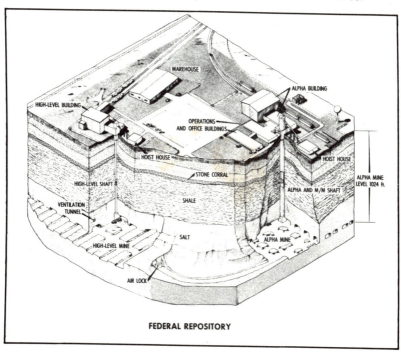

the waste will be monitored for five years, after which time the project's success or failure can be assessed.

Over the years, a number of other ideas for high-level waste disposal have been proposed and—at least temporarily—abandoned. One was disposal in space, in which sealed containers of radioactive material would be sent up into distant orbits. This would be an expensive and risky operation, as problems on the launchpad or in space could expose the earth and atmosphere to radiation. Another suggestion, burying waste under the Antarctic ice sheets, would risk irradiating that area and the surrounding sea. A much safer idea, which would render disposal unnecessary, is to bombard radioactive waste with subatomic particles to transform it into less harmful isotopes; unfortunately, this attractive proposal awaits still unrealized technology.

MILL TAILINGS

Mill tailings, left over when ore is refined and processed, constitute yet another waste category—the largest by volume of any form of radioactive waste. Only 1% of uranium ore contains uranium—the remainder is left on-site as sandlike residue. These tailings are generally left outdoors in huge piles, where they blow around, releasing radioactive thorium, radium, and radon into the surrounding air and water. By 1989, some 140 million tons of mill tailings had accumulated in the United States alone, with 10 to 15 million tons added each year. Although their radiation is generally less concentrated than that in other forms of waste, some of the isotopes in these tailings are long-lived and can be hazardous for many thousands of years.

Until their radioactive risk was known, mill tailings were sometimes used as foundation and building materials, especially in western states. Congress authorized cleanup funds for a Colorado site in 1972 and enacted the Uranium Mill Tailings Control Act in 1978, under which the DOE was required to take responsibility for the tailings at inactive sites; those at active mills became the responsibility of the mill operators. These monitored sites are generally safer, although some groundwater contamination still occurs at them. The NRC has recommended that tailings be stored underground in clay pits, far from population centers.

LOW-LEVEL WASTE

Low-level wastes are usually defined in terms of what they are not: They are not spent fuel, mill tailings, reprocessed materials, or transuranic materials. Low-level waste includes the remainder of radioactive wastes and materials generated in power plants, such as contaminated reactor water, plus those created in medical laboratories, hospitals, and industry. Wastes in this category usually, although not always, release smaller amounts of radiation for a shorter amount of time. "Low level" does not mean "not dangerous," however. Although its radioactivity is usually less concentrated than that of high-level waste, low-level waste can, depending on its content, be dangerous for up to tens of thousands of years.

About 54% of low-level wastes by volume—and 99% of the radioactive content of these wastes—come from reactors, whose waste can be divided into fuel and nonfuel categories. Fuel wastes are fission products that leak out of fuel rods and into cooling water. Nonfuel wastes, or *activation products*, result when stray neutrons bombard anything in the core other than fuel—such as the reactor vessel itself—and cause them to become radioactive. Even though less than 5% of low-level nuclear plant wastes come from this activation, such wastes are more radioactive than all the low-level fission wastes combined.

The remainder of low-level wastes comes from industry and institutional sources, including pharmaceutical plants, universities, and medical facilities. Instead of going to low-level waste dumps, these wastes are often kept on-site for the short time—sometimes just a matter of days or weeks—it takes for them to decay to safe levels; they are then disposed of in sanitary

Barrels of contaminated material outside a uranium processing plant in Ohio. On-site storage space for nuclear waste is becoming increasingly scarce.

landfills. It is likely that liquid wastes are literally poured down the drain, whether or not they are still radioactive.

Low-level-waste landfills were first built in the 1960s. In near-surface land burial, containers of waste fill a trench and are covered and surrounded by compacted earth. There are currently three government-licensed, privately managed burial grounds in the United States to which most commercial low-level waste materials emitting detectable amounts of radiation are sent. These are in Beatty, Nevada; Barnwell, South Carolina; and Richland, Washington. Three other landfills, located in Kentucky, Illinois, and New York, are currently inactive due to severe waste-containment problems and radioactive leakage. Waste containers in near-surface landfills are prone to corrosion, particularly in moist climates.

Landfills provide a false sense of comfort because they are "out of sight, out of mind." One worthwhile alternative to the landfill is the above-ground facility, in which radioactive waste is continually monitored and prevented from leaching into water. A Canadian utility company called Ontario Hydro stores decaying waste in a concrete building fitted with fire extinguishing, ventilation, and internal drainage systems. Another alternative to landfills is to store waste at existing nuclear plant sites.

More control of low-level wastes would also be gained by the further development of waste volume–reduction techniques and the separation and classification of waste by the length of time it will remain radioactive. Long-lived low-level wastes might be better stored with high-level wastes in permanent repositories. A number of techniques can be used to minimize low-level waste volume. Radioactive liquids may be filtered, and the trapped waste disposed of in sealed drums. Reactor water is often purified using ion exchange, in which tiny electrically charged plastic beads attract radioactive ions. The beads, now radioactive, must then be disposed of. Liquid wastes can also be evaporated to remove water, leaving behind radioactive sludge for disposal. Solidification in concrete, asphalt, or polyethylene drums is another waste-reduction strategy. Solid wastes such as contaminated clothing may be be incinerated, leaving a smaller volume of radioactive waste ash. The air in which this procedure takes place is filtered before being released into the environment. Radioactive trash may also be compacted to one-tenth of its original volume.

As one way of reducing the amount of radioactive waste requiring special disposal, the NRC announced in 1990 that it would consider certain types of radioactive waste—including smoke detectors, irradiated laboratory animal carcasses, items of clothing, parts from decommissioned power plants, and sealed radioactive sources from medical equipment—below regulatory concern. As a result, these wastes can be recycled into consumer goods, incinerated without the use of filters, or disposed of in municipal garbage dumps. The NRC believes its new policy will free it and its licensees "to focus on the regulation of materials that pose much more significant risks to the public." The NRC also sometimes grants case-by-case exemptions—for example, permitting cleaning sludge from cooling water at a reactor to be plowed into open land. Critics fear that the high cost and difficulty of dealing with radioactive waste will lead to increased NRC waste reclassification and case-by-case exemption, resulting in more radiation "loose" in the environment.

The Low Level Radioactive Waste Policy Act of 1980 made individual states responsible for their own low-level wastes.

Under the act, states must establish their disposal capacity by 1993; they have the option to work alone or to form regional compacts with neighbors and share a jointly run site. Nine regional compacts currently exist, with the states of California, Texas, New York, and Vermont among those working independently.

There are a number of unresolved issues regarding disposal of low-level wastes. The current institutional control period (the amount of time a waste site must remain under guard after it has been filled and closed) is only 100 years. Yet the hazards presented by some low-level wastes can continue for thousands of years. What will keep future generations from uncovering and being contaminated by these substances? Also at issue regarding both low- and high-level wastes are decisions about site selection and disposal methods. Although urban areas consume the lion's share of nuclear-generated electricity, radioactive wastes are dumped in rural settings, where property values decline and public health is jeopardized.

The problem of radioactive waste disposal is not unique to the United States. Other countries are facing the same low-level waste dilemmas, and there is currently no known permanent high-level waste repository anywhere in the world. Although the hazards of radioactive waste are less visible than some other problems associated with nuclear energy—such as reactor accidents and nuclear weapons—they are no less dangerous, and decisions made concerning this waste will be felt far into the future.

NUCLEAR TRANSIT

Each year there are approximately 2 million shipments of radioactive materials in the United States alone. Two-thirds of these involve medical and industrial materials; radioactive materials used for commercial nuclear power production—including uranium ore, enriched fuel, fuel rods, and nuclear waste—constitute the remainder. Most shipments are of low-level waste, although the amount of high-level waste in transit will undoubtedly increase when a permanent repository is built.

Transporting all these materials presents a number of hazards. A leaking container could spew radioactive materials onto a highway; an automobile or train accident could result in widespread radiation contamination. Shipments are also vulnerable to theft or hijacking of materials used in weapons manufacture.

The NRC and the Department of Transportation work together to regulate transportation of radioactive materials. Containers have been designed to prevent radiation leaks and withstand impacts. The reliability of these containers is much debated, however; some have failed impact and fire-resistance tests.

Nearly 3,000 mishaps involving transported commercial nuclear materials occurred in the United States in the 1970s and 1980s. Information on incidents involving military shipments is classified by the government. Most of the known accidents involved low-level wastes and caused little damage or injury. Most experts agree, however, that further testing of containers is needed, as is strict monitoring of the manufacture and use of these containers and careful handling and routing of radioactive materials on the nation's highways.

There is also the question of the rights of individuals and communities to know when and where such shipments take place, if there is a real danger of an accident. With weapons-grade nuclear materials, security considerations would override local community interests. But for less critical nuclear materials and low-level wastes, the public's right to know may come into conflict with government agencies more concerned with adverse publicity than protection of citizens. The record of nuclear regulatory agencies in admitting to or revealing problems has been less than ideal.

A state-of-the-art container for transporting radioactive materials by rail.

An aerial view of the Chernobyl nuclear power plant several months after the disastrous accident there in 1986.

chapter 5

NUCLEAR ACCIDENTS

(A modern nuclear reactor contains the radiation equivalent of 1,000 Hiroshima bombs. That destructive power can be unleashed in accidents of various kinds, such as a meltdown or a gas or steam explosion inside the reactor containment structure. These and other disasters have occurred throughout the world in the past four decades at both commercial and military reactors as well as on ships, submarines, and even satellites. Thousands of smaller accidents take place at nuclear facilities each year, resulting in the exposure of workers to radiation and the loss of radioactive material into the environment.)

The most feared nuclear accident is a meltdown, in which the reactor core receives inadequate coolant, causing the fuel to overheat and melt. Molten fuel melts through the steel reactor vessel and the containment structure, contaminating the surrounding environment. Initially it was thought that the molten fuel would continue to bore its way deep into the earth, hence the facetious phrase "China syndrome." (An old myth holds that a hole dug straight through the ground in the United States would eventually reach China.) Current belief is that the molten fuel would only make it several feet into the ground below the plant before being contained by glassifying soil. The escaped radiation could nevertheless contaminate a huge area if it reached surrounding groundwater.

Studies estimating casualties and damages from major accidents such as meltdowns have been conducted since the nuclear industry's inception. Over the years, these estimates have become increasingly pessimistic. A 1982 report by the Sandia National Laboratory in New Mexico predicted that a worst-case accident in the United States could cause between 50,000 and 100,000 immediate deaths, 10,000 to 40,000 subsequent deaths from cancer, and at least $100 billion in damages. As of 1990, federal compensation for a single nuclear accident was limited to $7 billion.

Although no nuclear plant accidents have caused this much devastation yet, many have been severe and in some cases have come very close to a worst-case scenario. The following are just some of the more serious incidents that have occurred worldwide since the advent of nuclear power.

CHELYABINSK-40

One of the earliest nuclear disasters occurred in the Soviet Union in late 1957 or early 1958, at the Chelyabinsk-40 facility near the city of Kyshtym in the Ural Mountains. Little is known about the accident, which probably took place at a plutonium-processing plant. In 1988, Soviet officials finally acknowledged that an accident had in fact occurred. A tank holding radioactive gases exploded, contaminating thousands of square miles around the facility. Whether or not there were casualties is unknown. The region around Chelyabinsk is now sealed off, and the names of more than 30 towns in the area have disappeared from Soviet maps.

WINDSCALE

The year 1957 witnessed another major accident at a reprocessing plant named Windscale (now called Sellafield), north of Liverpool, England. In a routine maintenance procedure at a reactor used to produce plutonium for nuclear weapons, the graphite moderator overheated. Faulty temperature indicators did not alert plant operators to the problem in time, and the fuel ignited. The reactor was flooded with water and the fire was eventually contained, but a large amount of radiation escaped, contaminating 200 square miles (516 square kilometers) of the surrounding countryside. Two million liters of milk contaminated with radioactive iodine were thrown out in nearby rivers and the Atlantic Ocean in the weeks following the accident. The accident at Windscale is estimated to have caused hundreds of cases of cancer and possibly birth defects; the incidence of leukemia in the area is now approximately 10 times the national average.

BROWN'S FERRY

A near tragedy occurred on March 22, 1975, at the Brown's Ferry nuclear plant near Decatur, Alabama, when a maintenance worker used a candle—against regulations—to test for air leaks around electrical cables and started a fire that spread to the reactor. Both the primary and several backup core-cooling systems were knocked out; a supplemental pump provided just

Six thousand gallons of radiation-contaminated milk were poured away daily for weeks at this dairy in Barrow-in-Furness, England, following the 1957 accident at the Windscale reprocessing plant.

enough water to the reactor core to prevent a meltdown. Although the Brown's Ferry accident was clearly caused by human error, it also raised questions about the effectiveness of cooling systems and led the NRC to require fire-safety changes at other plants.

THREE MILE ISLAND

The accident that began at Three Mile Island (TMI) Unit 2 on March 28, 1979, was the worst commercial nuclear reactor accident in the United States to date. TMI Unit 2, a pressurized-water reactor built by Babcock & Wilcox, had been in operation for less than four troubled months. Even though a similar Babcock

& Wilcox–built reactor at the Rancho Seco nuclear plant in California had a poor safety record, TMI Unit 2 went on-line in December 1978, largely so that its owner, the General Public Utilities Company (the parent of Metropolitan Edison, the local electrical utility), could qualify for millions of dollars in tax breaks. The NRC was not unaware of possible safety problems—in early 1979, an NRC inspector had recommended that all operational Babcock & Wilcox pressurized-water reactors in the United States be evaluated for problems—but no action was taken.

The accident at Three Mile Island occurred during the routine cleaning of a polisher. Polishers remove impurities from cooling water to prevent various chemicals from coming in contact with a reactor's components, which might be affected adversely. During the procedure, a cooling system water pump failed, which automatically halted the turbine. That stopped electricity output, but the reactor itself was still putting out full power. Temperatures rose in the cooling circuit. A safety valve automatically opened to cool the circuit, and the reactor scrammed and shut down operation. The system had reacted properly thus far.

Once the circuit cooled down, the safety valve should have closed automatically. The control room console incorrectly indicated that this had happened. Instead, the valve remained open, causing the system to steadily lose pressure and coolant. Control room operators were relying on a backup cooling system to keep the reactor core covered with water. Assuming that the backup system was adequate, they turned off most of the emergency coolant pumps. What the operators did not know was that their backup system was turned off as well. What little coolant was left in the system turned into steam, partially exposing the reactor core. Temperatures within the reactor shot up, fuel rods ruptured, and meltdown began.

A few hours after the accident started, a general emergency was declared by the TMI manager, based on 20,000-rad-per-hour radiation readings from under the containment dome. The NRC refused to believe the radiation readings from the plant and attributed them to instrument error. Unfounded faith in nuclear power technology blinded many experts to the possibility that something was seriously wrong at TMI Unit 2.

With erroneous information displayed on the control room console and safety systems unwittingly disabled, operators had no idea of what was really happening, nor did Metropolitan Edison and the NRC. Six hours after the accident started, an NRC division head was convinced that the reactor core had begun meltdown. Babcock & Wilcox engineers and engineers at the utility's parent company deduced that the core was uncovered, too. They convinced operators to increase reactor pressure and coolant, which ultimately averted a complete meltdown.

A sample of cooling water could not be taken until two days later, on March 30. It contained so much radiation that the damaged fuel theory was confirmed. At that point, plant operators were primarily concerned with containing the radiation. The reactor's containment vessel was loaded with radioactive water, and thousands of gallons had been pumped to a less shielded auxiliary building. Radioactive gas had also flooded a water supply tank. In the process of transferring this gas to another tank, some of it was released through venting to the air and was carried toward nearby towns by the wind.

That day, Pennsylvania governor Richard Thornburgh opted to evacuate young children and pregnant women from a five-mile radius surrounding the plant. More than 150,000 residents of local townships within 15 miles of the plant voluntarily fled—on average traveling 100 miles out of the area and remaining away for several days.

As radiation levels began to fall, it became possible to enter the containment building by stages to see what had actually occurred. No one was prepared for what was revealed by the remote-control television cameras lowered into the reactor vessel. The fuel assemblies had burst open, and, along with a few hundred tons of radioactive rubble, the vessel also contained 20 tons—more than half the core—of melted uranium fuel, which

This photograph of the 1979 accident at the Three Mile Island nuclear power plant in Pennsylvania shows radioactive steam being vented to cool the reactor.

had cooled and hardened. For uranium fuel to melt, temperatures of at least 5100°F (2815°C) must be reached. The fuel had almost completely breached the eight-inch-thick steel reactor vessel. A total meltdown was prevented only by a last-minute rush of cooling water.

It is unclear how much radiation escaped into the atmosphere during the accident. Although plant vent stacks were equipped with radiation monitors, these were damaged by steam and rendered useless. Because radiation-monitoring devices were inadequate, a systematic effort to collect radiation information did not take place. An estimated comparison of radiation in the core

Workers in protective clothing examine radioactive wastes spilled in Richland, Washington, en route to a burial site.

before and after the accident—which would have indicated the amount of escaped radiation—was not performed. Critics feel that the NRC and Metropolitan Edison downplayed the accident's severity and that public safety precautions were not taken in a timely manner.

Radioactive water was dumped into the Susquehanna River, and plumes of radioactive gas escaped the building, but utility and NRC officials claimed that only minor emissions occurred and that dairy products and local produce did not contain high levels of fallout. Local individuals and researchers, however, picked up high radiation readings from the air and on local wildlife and farm animals. Dairy farmers in the surrounding countryside reported that many of their animals died soon after the accident. Some local residents have since been diagnosed with cancer and leukemia, although whether this can be attributed to the accident is uncertain.

Evaluations of the health effects of the Three Mile Island incident have differed. A 1981 study by Dr. George Tokuhata, director of epidemiology for the Pennsylvania State Department of Health, concluded that the accident did not have a significant effect on the physical health of local residents. But several scientists have criticized this report, and a 1980 study by Dr. Gordon MacLeod, the Pennsylvania State Department of Health secretary, showed a strong increase in infant mortality and an unusually large number of babies born with severe thyroid disorders, both of which are signs of fetal radiation exposure. It is still too early to tell what the accident's long-term effects will be. As of 1989, 2,000 lawsuits had been filed by residents of Dauphin County seeking compensation for medical problems caused by the accident. The plant's owner has settled some cases out of court with the provision that the plaintiffs not discuss the settlement.

By the end of 1990, the main task of removing the tons of radioactive material from the core at TMI Unit 2 was almost completed; contaminated water used to flood the reactor building is still being evaporated. Robots are cleaning areas too dangerous for humans to enter. Nuclear waste is taken by railroad to a site near Idaho Falls, Idaho. The cleanup, waste storage, entombment, and decommissioning is expected to cost at least $2 billion.

CHERNOBYL

The first clue about the disaster at the Chernobyl reactor complex, located on the Pripet River about 80 miles (130 kilometers) from the city of Kiev in the Soviet Union, came on April 28, 1986, 3 days into the meltdown. Technicians at the Forsmark nuclear reactor outside of Stockholm, Sweden, were reading abnormally high levels of radiation inside and around the plant, on workers, and in soil and vegetation samples. Other Scandinavian countries were showing similarly high readings. Winds were coming from the direction of the Soviet Union, but no information was available from the Soviet government. Later that day, an official announcement of an accident at the Chernobyl power station was telecast from Moscow.

The accident—considered the worst in commercial nuclear reactor history—began late on the night of April 25, when power station operators undertook a test of one of the turbines connected to Unit 4, a boiling-water, graphite-moderated reactor that had performed flawlessly since going on-line in 1983. The operators were trying to determine if under power blackout

Public opposition to nuclear power has mounted in recent decades in the wake of the accidents at Three Mile Island and Chernobyl.

conditions there would be enough energy production to keep turbines spinning for the 45 seconds it takes for emergency generators to begin working. They disconnected the emergency core-cooling system, powered down to 1% of operating power, turned off other safety systems, and withdrew most of the control rods.

Power output rose dramatically, reaching 100 times normal levels. Fuel disintegrated and evaporated the cooling water. The buildup of steam exploded the reactor's lid. (Unlike commercial power reactors in the United States, the Chernobyl reactor was not built with a containment structure.) Flaming debris from the reactor showered over the complex's buildings, setting them on fire. As cooling water reacted with the graphite core, hydrogen gas built up, causing a second explosion that sent radioactive material one mile up into the sky.

Meanwhile, fires raged throughout the reactor complex. It took 10 days to control the burning core. Several thousand tons of radiation-absorbing materials such as boron and lead were dropped into the exposed reactor. Nitrogen was pumped under the reactor vessel to cool it, and a huge concrete slab was placed below the reactor to keep molten fuel from burning through. By the end of 1986, the plant was completely entombed in a steel-and-concrete-reinforced radiation-containment structure. It is uncertain, however, whether or not this will provide sufficient shielding over time.

Ultimately, 31 firemen and plant workers died of severe radiation exposure and burns. Within 2 days of the accident, close to 50,000 people had been evacuated from the town of Pripet. Eventually, more than 100,000 people and 86,000 head of cattle were removed from nearby villages and towns and permanently resettled elsewhere. For at least a month after the accident, all the buildings in Kiev were hosed down daily to remove radioactive particles. Approximately 1,000 square miles of land around the complex are permanently contaminated. Financial losses from the accident have been estimated at $10 billion.

Half of Chernobyl's fallout dropped within 30 or so miles of the complex. The remainder traveled in a radioactive cloud carried by prevailing winds over parts of the Soviet Union, Scandinavia, continental Europe, Great Britain, and Ireland. Smaller amounts of radiation were measured as far away as the United States and the Middle East. Public health precautions varied from country to country, depending on radiation levels and each country's acceptable limits. Milk from cows that had eaten contaminated grasses was banned in Poland and Scandinavian countries but not in Germany. Fruits and vegetables from the Soviet Union were banned in many countries. The French government gave very little advice to the public—French radiation standards for food and water are the lowest in Europe.

A U.S. Department of Energy study of Chernobyl's impact, performed by Marvin Goldman and colleagues at the University of California at Davis, predicted that Chernobyl will ultimately cause 40,000 cases of cancer worldwide, approximately one-third of them in the Soviet Union. This is a middle-of-the-road estimate; some researchers predict fewer cases of cancer, others more. The accident, horrible as it was, could have caused many more injuries. The radioactive cloud did not pass over Kiev and thus spared that city's 2.5 million inhabitants.

Chernobyl and other accidents in recent decades have created mounting public resistance worldwide to nuclear energy. It has been argued in the nuclear industry's defense that many accidents are prevented or their severity lessened because safeguards do in fact work. Advocates of nuclear power also suggest that lessons have been learned from these incidents that will prevent their recurrence in the future. Yet even though design changes and new safety precautions are being implemented in response to the various accidents that have occurred, some NRC officials still estimate a 45% chance of a Chernobyl-scale accident occurring in the United States by the year 2000; the likelihood that one will happen somewhere in the world before then is even higher.

The entrance to the Shoreham nuclear power plant on Long Island, New York; public opposition prevented the opening of the facility and as of 1991 it stood unused.

chapter 6

THE FUTURE OF NUCLEAR POWER

Whether promoting it or working against it, many people and organizations are involved in the controversy over nuclear power. Utility companies, power plant designers, parts manufacturers, building contractors, government and scientific agencies, industry groups, and antinuclear organizations all have a stake—as do all those on the sidelines—in either perpetuating the industry as it is, changing it, or shutting it down. To some, nuclear power is the most viable source of electricity to power the future; others support alternatives and feel hopeful that the nuclear industry is showing signs of demise, at least in the industrialized world.

Throughout the world, the costs of building and operating nuclear power plants are rising; the 1950s goal of nuclear energy–generated electricity "too cheap to meter" has clearly not been achieved. Newer U.S. nuclear plants generate electricity at an average cost of more than 13 cents per kilowatt-hour, more than twice that of coal-burning plants equipped with the latest air pollution–control equipment. This price does not even include most of the expenses of radioactive waste disposal and plant decommissioning.

Contributing to the price of nuclear power in some countries is that many reactors regularly experience long outages and are not operating anywhere close to full capacity. In the United States, pressurized-water reactors are functioning at only about 60% of capacity; in the United Kingdom and Sweden these reactors are performing at an even lower capacity. Canadian, Japanese, French, German, and Swiss pressurized-water reactors operate at a much higher capacity, thanks to more standardized designs and better overall management.

A new generation rallies against nuclear power at a demonstration in Washington, D.C.

Operating costs aside, the expense of nuclear energy in terms of medical costs of those suffering the effects of radiation has yet to be calculated; the cost of nuclear energy in terms of human lives *cannot* be calculated. The effects of nuclear power and radioactive waste disposal on human health are just beginning to be understood, as studies of exposure to low-level radiation explore its potential to cause cancer, leukemia, and genetic defects.

The accidents that have occurred in recent decades have contributed to the price tag of nuclear power and have fueled mounting public resistance to nuclear energy. According to a Harris poll conducted in 1988, 61% of the U.S. public opposed the construction of more nuclear power plants—as opposed to only about 30% a decade earlier. Numerous antinuclear organizations and industry watchdogs have become active worldwide (see Appendix).

NUCLEAR WEAPONS PROLIFERATION

Many feel the greatest hazard of nuclear power is its contribution to nuclear weapons proliferation. Even commercial power reactors provide the raw materials—plutonium and some uranium isotopes—for nuclear weapons. For example, although Canada's atomic program is devoted to the production of commercial energy, Canadian spent fuel is shipped to military reactor sites in the United States, where the plutonium is extracted for use in nuclear weapons.

In addition, when industrialized nations sell reactors to developing countries—and many do—they are potentially encouraging nuclear weapons proliferation. Commercial reactors can be converted to manufacture weapons-grade plutonium. Although signatories of the 1968 Nuclear Non-Proliferation Treaty have agreed not to develop nuclear weapons in return for help in building commercial power facilities, it is questionable whether this treaty can really be enforced. Moreover, the list of countries that have not signed the treaty but have, or are developing, nuclear weapons capability is growing fast—as is the amount of weapons-grade plutonium that is unaccounted for.

In *The Nuclear Barons,* authors Peter Pringle and James Spigelman conclude that the development of nuclear technology "was a stunning achievement of many clever men. What is in question now is not their cleverness but their wisdom." Splitting the atom to produce electricity is an incredible feat but a hazardous one, and efforts are under way both to improve nuclear fission technology and to cultivate safer alternatives. Energy strategies for the future include developing fusion reactors, investing in renewable energy sources, and increasing energy efficiency and conservation.

IMPROVING NUCLEAR POWER

The first generation of nuclear reactors are nearing the end of their operational life. In the United States, federal funds have been given to reactor manufacturers to come up with safer designs for the second generation. General Atomics is currently promoting a helium gas–cooled, graphite-moderated reactor. This type of reactor is already used extensively in France and England. Its purported safety advantage is that helium gas, unlike water, does not turn to steam and so is a more effective coolant.

Westinghouse has developed a pressurized-water reactor with safety devices that rely less on human intervention or moving parts that can malfunction. One new coolant method uses convection, a natural process whereby differences in temperature combined with the pull of gravity permit air to circulate and cool a reactor. There is also a general trend toward smaller reactors that are easier to cool, are built in clusters, and are run from one central control room. A preliminary assessment by the Union of Concerned Scientists, an industry watchdog, favors some of these design innovations, including natural features such as gravity and convection, but not others, such as multireactor control rooms.

A cancer patient is prepared for radiation therapy, a product of the nuclear age that has proved an invaluable tool in modern medicine.

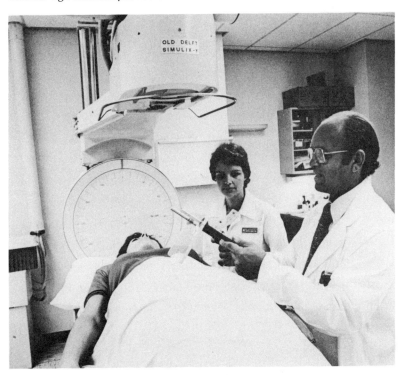

Improvements are also being pursued abroad. In 1991, Japan is expected to begin construction on the world's first advanced boiling-water reactor, also designed by General Electric. The design includes fiber-optic wiring, a larger reactor core, increased automation, additional backup systems, and an improved water circulation system. The French are beginning to develop second-generation pressurized-water reactors, and Great Britain plans to replace old gas-cooled reactors with new pressurized-water reactors. These various new designs may offer significant improvements over existing reactors, but construction, maintenance, management, and personnel training must also be improved. And no matter how well reactors work, the problem of radioactive waste disposal remains unsolved.

FUSION

The generation of electricity from fusion reactors has been a goal of scientists since the 1940s. Fusion reactors duplicate the sun's activities, in which temperatures of 14 million degrees Celsius and intense gravitational pressure press atoms so close together that their nuclei join and release energy. A fusion reactor cannot re-create crushing gravitational pressures and so compensates by operating at temperatures of at least a hundred million degrees Celsius. This blazing heat converts the hydrogen isotopes deuterium and tritium into energy-releasing plasma, a cloud of electrically charged particles that no vessel can contain. Instead, magnetic fields are used to "hold" the plasma in place.

Controlled artificial fusion has so far proved elusive. The most advanced project to date, the Tokamak Fusion Test Reactor at Princeton University, has been able to achieve a world-record temperature of 400 million degrees Celsius. Now that such high temperatures have been attained, scientists' attentions have turned to creating and containing dense, energy-charged plasma. This will require building another fusion machine, the Compact Ignition Tokamak, at an estimated cost of $1 billion. It is envisioned that by the beginning of the 21st century the final test stages will take place in the International Thermonuclear Reactor, a joint venture by the United States, Japan, European countries, and the Soviet Union. *If* all goes well, the world's first fusion reactor could be up and running as early as the year 2040.

Is all the money and effort required to test the possibilities of fusion justifiable? The advantages of fusion are that its fuel—heavy water—is easily produced from sea water, relatively inexpensive, and virtually unlimited. Skeptics argue, however, that fusion reactors will be expensive, fragile, and subject to frequent breakdowns. Fusion's radioactive materials and by-products are another important consideration. At best, fusion is billions of dollars and half a century away. As of 1990, the federal government had not yet decided whether to fund the Compact Ignition Tokamak.

RENEWABLE ENERGY SOURCES

Energy from the sun, earth, wind, and water can be used to produce electricity in processes that are more environmentally safe than those involving coal, oil, or nuclear power. Increasingly high oil prices, environmental damage from burning fossil fuels, the shrinking supplies of these fuels, and the hazards of nuclear energy production make renewable energy options increasingly attractive.

At Beverly High School in Beverly, Massachusetts, electricity is generated from sunlight by photovoltaic cells, which provide about 10% of the school's electricity.

According to a UN-sponsored study by the Advisory Group on Greenhouse Gases released in 1990, serious environmental damage from global warming will become apparent sooner than was once expected, beginning early in the 21st century. The study made several recommendations for slowing this trend, including instituting stricter energy efficiency standards, planting forests, and increasing the use of natural gas and alternative energy sources.

Most forms of renewable energy, including *biomass, solar-thermal,* wind, and *hydropower,* are loosely considered *solar* because they tap the sun's energy, either directly or indirectly. Other forms rely on heat from within the earth or ocean or draw on energy from ocean tides and currents.

All of these sources are widely available and—if managed wisely—are potentially cheap, virtually inexhaustible, and safe for the environment.

Biomass—wood, crop remains, and animal dung—is an important energy source, particularly in the Third World. New technology is enabling more efficient use of these materials. In Brazil, for example, fermented sugarcane is used to make a type of alcohol called ethanol, which can be used as fuel for cars and to supply factories with electricity. Brazilian researchers are experimenting with ways to generate electricity from biomass on a large scale as well. In the United States, corn is used in the same way as sugarcane to produce ethanol for use as a gasoline extender. One drawback to this new use of biomass is that it diverts valuable organic soil fertilizers for use as fuel.

Hydropower refers to electricity generated from falling water, usually by means of large dams. In 1987, this energy source provided 31% of the electricity produced in developing countries and 17% of that generated in industrialized nations, and its use is increasing. Hydropower is not without drawbacks, however: Water diversion to create dams often displaces people and animals and destroys habitats.

A number of countries, including Norway, Great Britain, India, and Japan, have committed research funds to wave power. In this form of energy production, a water chamber built along a shoreline is connected to an airway, turbine, and generator. When a wave comes in, water fills the chamber and pushes air into the airway, where it drives a turbine. As the wave recedes, a vacuum created in the airway pulls air back through the turbine, which is driven regardless of the airflow's direction.

A pilot wave-powered plant at Islay, an island on Scotland's western coast, produces 40 kilowatts a day, which meets the electrical needs of the small island community. If more energy becomes needed, multiple small units could be installed. The Islay plant and another 40-kilowatt venture in a small fishing village in Japan are among the more successful wave-power projects. In 1988, a Norwegian wave-power device was destroyed in a storm, and a project in India was canceled because waves on the site were not strong enough. A large-scale application of wave power under way in France may require adaptation because environmentalists claim that its large barriers disrupt marine life.

Wind power is another promising renewable energy source. A new wind-powered turbine similar to a windmill is currently being developed by U.S. Windpower in Livermore, California. The turbine, which has three 54-foot-long blades, is connected to a 300-kilowatt generator. The device functions in both high and variable winds. Thousands of "wind farms" have been built in the past 2 decades, primarily in California, where 85% of the devices installed worldwide in the 1980s were built, and Denmark. A number of other countries have large wind-power projects in the works.

Solar-thermal energy works on the principle of trapping the sun's heat in a liquid or gas that can then be pumped through a building to heat it. Sometimes the liquid or gas transfers heat to another area for storage. Solar panels can also boil water into steam, for direct use or to generate electricity, although the steam cannot be stored or transported long distances.

Solar photovoltaic cells convert sunlight into a low-voltage electrical current. Such devices have already been used extensively on space capsules and satellites. On earth, the solar cells are carefully arranged in *arrays* (groups of lines) to maximize their electrical output. Photovoltaic cells are not yet cost-effective but with increasing use would become more economical. The Soviet Union is building a new factory to produce photovoltaic cells for use in remote areas of that country. The Soviet plan is to begin with 2 megawatts' worth of solar cells per year (enough electricity for 1,000 households) and eventually expand to 100–150 megawatts.
  Geothermal energy harnesses the heat of the earth's interior. Volcanoes, hot springs, and geysers are geothermal sources. They can heat a liquid, such as water, that can then be

Dairy cattle graze a stone's throw from a uranium processing plant in Ohio.

used directly for heating or converted into steam to drive an electrical generator. More than 130 geothermal plants are operating worldwide, in such countries as Iceland, the United States, New Zealand, and Italy. A drawback to this energy source is that water from geothermal sources sometimes contains salt and mineral pollutants. Also, geothermal plants can release harmful gases.

The percentage of energy produced from renewable sources is increasing worldwide. In the United States, that percentage—about 9% in 1988—is expected to double by the year 2000, according to the Global Tomorrow Coalition. In addition, the expense of renewable energy is declining; the cost of electricity from wind power and solar cells, for example, is now competitive with that generated by nuclear power and is expected to be cheaper within just a few years.

ENERGY EFFICIENCY

The least expensive of all energy "sources" are energy conservation, or using as little as possible, and improved energy efficiency. In the past two decades, industries in many nations—most notably Japan—have greatly improved their energy efficiency by means of technological and other improvements. Domestic energy efficiency can be improved as well, by insulating homes and using more efficient appliances and lighting and heating devices. A recent World Resources Institute study estimates that a family that employs these strategies will use only one-fourth of the energy required by a "typical" household. Another important energy efficiency measure is designing automobiles to increase the number of miles they can travel per gallon of gasoline.

Does the world need nuclear power, or can its energy needs be met by using alternative energy sources and increased energy conservation and efficiency? And how will this question be answered years from now, when fossil fuel reserves have been depleted? Perhaps an apt symbol of the current indecision and disagreement surrounding this issue is the Shoreham nuclear power plant on Long Island, in New York. Virtually completed in 1984 at a cost of more than $5 billion, Shoreham has yet to operate. Opposition from worried citizens and local and state officials—who believe Long Island could not be evacuated quickly enough in case of a serious accident—have stalled efforts to open the plant. The utility company that constructed Shoreham and New York State have worked out an agreement to dismantle the plant, but the NRC has not yet given permission for total dismantlement, and local nuclear power proponents are still pushing to use Shoreham for nuclear power production. Meanwhile, the almost bankrupt utility's customers are being charged higher rates for their electricity to pay for the facility.

If the nuclear power industry is to survive without jeopardizing the public and the environment, many problems must be solved. A way must be found to reprocess uranium safely so that it will last longer, plant design and operation must be improved to reduce radioactive emissions and prevent accidents, and safe waste-disposal methods and locations must be found. Whether all these problems can be solved remains to be seen; whether humankind can afford to continue using nuclear energy *without* solving them is doubtful.

APPENDIX: FOR MORE INFORMATION

Organizations

Edison Electric Institute
701 Pennsylvania Avenue
Washington, DC 20006
(202) 508-5000

Global Tomorrow Coalition
1325 G Street NW
Washington, DC 20005
(202) 628-4016

Greenpeace USA
Main Office
1436 U Street NW
Washington, DC 20009
(202) 462-1177

Nuclear Information and
  Resource Service
1424 16th Street NW
Suite 601
Washington, DC 20036
(202) 328-0002

Public Citizen Critical Mass
  Energy Project
215 Pennsylvania Avenue SE
Washington, DC 20003
(202) 546-4996

Radioactive Waste Campaign
7 West Street
Warwick, NY 10990
(914) 986-1115

SANE/FREEZE
711 G Street SE
Washington, DC 20003
(202) 546-7100

Union of Concerned Scientists
26 Church Street
Cambridge, MA 02238
(617) 547-5552

U.S. Public Interest Research
  Group
215 Pennsylvania Avenue SE
Washington, DC 20003
(202) 546-9707

U.S. Government Agencies

U.S. Council for Energy
  Awareness
Suite 400
1776 I Street NW
Washington, DC 20006-2495
(202) 293-0770

U.S. Department of Energy
Energy Information
  Administration
Forrestal Building
Washington, DC 20585
(202) 586-8800

U.S. Environmental Protection
  Agency

401 M Street SW
Washington, DC 20460
(202) 382-2090

U.S. Nuclear Regulatory
  Commission
Washington, DC 20555
(301) 492-7000
(Baltimore, MD)

FURTHER READING

Bertell, Rosalie. *No Immediate Danger.* Summertown, TN: The Book Publishing Company, 1985.

Croall, Stephen. *Nuclear Power for Beginners.* New York: Random House, 1983.

Ford, Daniel F. *Three Mile Island: Thirty Minutes to Meltdown.* New York: Penguin Books, 1982.

Freeman, Leslie J. *Nuclear Witnesses: Insiders Speak Out.* New York: Norton, 1981.

Gale, Robert Peter, and Thomas Hauser. *Final Warning: The Legacy of Chernobyl.* New York: Warner Books, 1988.

Global Tomorrow Coalition. *The Global Ecology Handbook: What You Can Do About the Environmental Crisis.* Edited by Walter H. Corson. Boston: Beacon Press, 1990.

Gould, Jay M., and Benjamin A. Goldman. *Deadly Deceit: Low Level Radiation, High Level Cover-up.* New York: Four Walls Eight Windows, 1990.

Lowrance, William W. *Of Acceptable Risk.* Los Altos, CA: Kaufmann, 1976.

McKay, Alwyn. *The Making of the Atomic Age.* New York: Oxford University Press, 1984.

May, John. *The Greenpeace Book of the Nuclear Age: The Hidden History, the Human Cost.* New York: Pantheon Books, 1989.

Miller, G. Tyler, Jr. *Living in the Environment: An Introduction to Environmental Science.* 6th ed. Belmonth, CA: Wadsworth, 1990.

Morrone, Joseph G., and Edward J. Woodhouse. *The Demise of Nuclear Energy?* New Haven: Yale University Press, 1989.

Murray, Raymond L. *Understanding Radioactive Waste.* Columbus, OH: Battelle Press, 1989.

Nader, Ralph, and John Abbotts. *The Menace of Atomic Energy.* New York: Norton, 1979.

Poch, David I. *Radiation Alert.* Toronto: Doubleday Canada, 1985.

Pringle, Peter, and James Spigelman. *The Nuclear Barons.* New York: Holt, Rinehart & Winston, 1981.

Radioactive Waste Campaign. *Deadly Defense: Military Radioactive Landfills.* New York: Radioactive Waste Campaign, 1988.

Resnikoff, Marvin. *Living Without Landfills.* New York: Radioactive Waste Campaign, 1987.

Rhodes, Richard. *The Making of the Atomic Bomb.* New York: Simon & Schuster, 1988.

Stephens, Mark. *Three Mile Island.* New York: Random House, 1980.

Stobaugh, Robert, and Daniel Yergin, eds. *Energy Future.* New York: Ballantine Books, 1979.

Sweet, William. *The Nuclear Age.* Washington, DC: Congressional Quarterly, 1988.

Weinberg, Steve. *The Discovery of Subatomic Particles.* New York: Scientific American, 1983.

GLOSSARY

alpha particle Radiation in the form of a subatomic particle composed of two protons and two neutrons.

atom The smallest characteristic component of the elements, consisting of a nucleus containing positively charged protons and uncharged neutrons, around which negatively charged electrons orbit.

beta particle Radiation in the form of a high-speed electron.

breeder reactor Type of nuclear reactor that produces more fuel than it consumes by converting unfissionable uranium into fissionable plutonium.

chain reaction The process by which one atomic fission releases extra neutrons that then cause more fissions, releasing more free neutrons, creating a self-sustaining reaction.

control rods Neutron-absorbing rods inserted into the nuclear reactor core to control the rate of fission.

coolant A substance, such as water, used in nuclear reactors to carry the heat created by fusion away from the reactor core.

core The central part of the reactor, containing the fuel assemblies and control rods.

decommissioning The cleanup process that occurs when a nuclear plant is taken out of service.

electromagnetic waves Energy-transmitting oscillations, or vibrations, in electric and magnetic fields, ranging from radio waves to gamma rays. The higher the frequency and the shorter the wavelength, the more destructive the wave.

fission The splitting of an atomic nucleus, resulting in the release of a great amount of energy.

fusion The joining together of atomic nuclei, which releases energy.

half-life The time required for half the atoms in a sample of a radioisotope to decay.

high-level waste Nuclear wastes, including spent fuel, that are usually highly radioactive for hundreds of thousands of years.

isotopes Atoms of the same element that contain the same number of protons but a different number of neutrons.

light-water reactor The most common type of reactor worldwide, in which ordinary water is used as both coolant and moderator and which requires enriched uranium fuel; includes both boiling-water and pressurized-water reactors.

low-level waste Radioactive materials, such as contaminated reactor water and medical waste, that are generally less radioactive than high-level waste and are radioactive for a shorter period of time.

meltdown A nuclear accident in which the uranium fuel in a reactor core overheats and melts, potentially releasing large amounts of radiation into the surrounding environment.

moderator A substance, such as heavy water or graphite, used in nuclear reactors to slow down neutrons, enabling them to penetrate uranium nuclei more easily, thereby causing fission.

rad Radiation absorbed dose; a measurement of the amount of radiation deposited in body tissue.

radiation Potentially destructive subatomic particles and rays emitted from an unstable atom's nucleus.

radioactive decay The spontaneous disintegration of an atomic nucleus, during which process radiation is emitted.

radioisotope Radioactive isotope.

rem Roentgen equivalent man; a measurement of the biological impact of radiation.

reprocessing Procedure in which spent fuel is treated to extract and reuse fissionable uranium and plutonium, reducing the volume and radioactivity of the remaining waste.

scram Emergency procedure in which all control rods are fully inserted into a reactor core to prevent a fuel meltdown.

spent fuel Highly radioactive used nuclear reactor fuel.

INDEX

Activation products, 66
ALARA (As Low As Reasonably Achievable), 55
Alpha particles, 33, 35
Atomic Energy Act of 1954, 15
    Price-Anderson amendment, 16
Atomic Energy Commission (AEC), 15, 16, 51
Atomic Energy Control Board (Canada), 51
Atomic pile, 14
Atoms, 13, 23, 25–37
    parts, 13, 25–27
"Atoms for Peace," 15
Austria, 23

Babcock & Wilcox Company, 44, 76–78
Background radiation, 35
Barnwell, South Carolina, 67
Beatty, Nevada, 67
Becquerel, Antoine-Henri, 27
Belgium, 16
Beta particles, 33
Binding force, 26–27, 29
Biomass, 19, 94–95
Birth defects, 36, 75, 81, 89
Brown's Ferry, 75–76

Canada, 16, 46, 51, 88, 89
Cancer, 18, 31, 32–33, 36, 47, 74, 75, 81, 85, 89

CANDU (Canadian Deuterium Uranium reactor), 46
Cap de la Hague, 50
Carbon dioxide, 19, 43
Carbon-14, 35
Carlsbad, New Mexico, 63
Carter, Jimmy, 50
Chadwick, James, 28
Chain reaction, 14, 29
Chelyabinsk-40, 74–75
Chernobyl, 22, 82–85
Chicago, University of, 14, 30
China syndrome, 73
Coal, 18, 19, 22, 93
Colorado, 40, 65
Columbia University, 29
Compact Ignition Tokamak, 93
Contamination, 52, 58, 84, 85. *See also* Emissions
Coolant, 44, 46, 47, 60, 73, 76, 77–78, 80, 90
Critical mass, 29
Curie, Marie, 28
Curie, Pierre, 28
Curie (measure), 55
Czechoslovakia, 23

Decommissioning, 22, 50–51, 82
Decontamination, 50
Denmark, 96
Department of Energy, U.S., 19, 52, 59, 60, 61–63, 65, 85
Department of Transportation, U.S., 52

Dismantlement, 51, 99
DNA (deoxyribonucleic acid), 32, 33

Einstein, Albert, 29
Eisenhower, Dwight D., 15
Electricity
    coal-generated, 18, 19, 20
    hydroelectric, 18
    natural gas–generated, 18, 19
    nuclear-generated, 14, 15, 16, 17–18, 52–53
    production, 39
    sources, 14, 15, 16, 17–18, 19, 20
Electromagnetic waves, 27, 34
    gamma rays, 34, 35. *See also* X rays
Emissions, 20, 35, 44–45, 47, 49, 58, 61, 64, 65, 67, 74, 78, 80–82, 84
Energy
    alternative sources, 93, 99
    definition, 13
    nonrenewable sources, 19
    percentage provided by nuclear power, 19
    renewable sources, 23, 93–98
    types, 13
Energy Research and Development Administration, 51–52
England, 50, 90
Entombment, 50–51, 82, 83
Environmental Protection Agency (EPA), 55, 61, 63
Ethanol, 95
Europe, 28, 29, 84, 85, 93

Fat Man, 31
Fermi, Enrico, 14, 28, 29, 30, 31
Fission, 13, 14, 27, 28, 39, 42–43, 44, 48
    products, 42, 46, 48, 60, 65
Flowers Report, 59
Forsmark, 82
France, 16, 17, 40, 46, 47, 50, 85, 88, 90, 92, 96
Fuel
    fossil, 19, 23, 39, 93, 99
    nuclear, 42
Fuel rods, 14, 40, 48, 57, 60–61, 65, 78
Fusion, 13–14, 90, 92–93

General Electric Company, 44, 92
General Public Utilities Company, 77
Genetic damage, 32–35, 89. *See also* Birth defects
Geologic disposal, 62
Geothermal energy, 97–98
Germany, 23, 85, 88
Global warming, 19–20, 94
Great Britain, 16, 46, 84, 92, 95

Hahn, Otto, 28
Half-life, 27
Hanford Nuclear Reservation, 22
Harris poll, 89
Hiroshima, Japan, 14, 31, 35
Hydrogen, 43, 83
Hydrological cycle, 58
Hydropower, 94–95. *See also* Electricity
Hyperthyroidism, 19

Iceland, 98

India, 23, 95
International Atomic Energy
    Agency, 15
International Thermonuclear
    Reactor, 93
Isotopes, 27
Italy, 28, 98

Japan, 23, 88, 92, 93, 95, 96, 98
Joliot-Curie, Frédéric, 28
Joliot-Curie, Irène, 28

Kentucky, 67
Kyshtym, Soviet Union, 74

Las Vegas, Nevada, 62
Leukemia, 32, 75, 81, 89
Little Boy, 31
Los Alamos Scientific Laboratory,
    31
Low Level Radioactive Waste
    Policy Act of 1980, 68

Manhattan Project, 29
Meitner, Lise, 28
Meltdown, 21, 43, 73, 74, 76, 78,
    80, 82
Metropolitan Edison, 77, 78, 81
Mill tailings, 57, 64–65
Moderators, 44, 46
Mortality, 22, 36, 74, 81, 84
Mothballing, 50–51

Nagasaki, Japan, 14, 31, 36
National Academy of Sciences,
    U.S., 58
National Research Council's
    Committee on the Biological
    Effects of Ionizing Radiation, 37

New Mexico, 31, 40, 74
New York, 61, 67, 69, 99
Norway, 95, 96
Nuclear accidents, 21, 69, 73–85
    cleanup, 22, 82
    cost, 16, 22, 52–55, 74, 82,
        84
Nuclear Barons, The (Pringle and
    Spigelman), 96
Nuclear energy, 13
    alternatives, 23, 96, 93–98
    cost, 16, 46, 47, 87
    development and
        promotion, 15
    effects on environment,
        19–20
    military uses, 15
    peaceful uses, 15
    safety, 17, 20, 36, 54
    as source of inexpensive
        electricity, 15, 16, 69, 87
    use by private industry, 15
    use in research, 19
Nuclear fuel cycle, 39–55
    back end processes, 48–50
    front end processes, 39–41
Nuclear Fuel Services, 49
Nuclear medicine, 18–19, 35
Nuclear Non-Proliferation Treaty
    (1968), 90
Nuclear power plants, 15, 16
    cost, 15, 89, 99
    cost-effectiveness, 23, 49
    decommissioning, 22,
        50–51, 82
    design, construction, and
        operation, 20, 23, 41–55,
        85, 90, 99
    maximum operating life, 50,
        51, 55, 90

public opposition to, 23, 87, 89, 99
Nuclear reactors 14, 30
   civilian use, 16
   light-water, 43, 46
   boiling-water, 44–45, 48, 82, 92
   breeder, 19, 46–47
   gas-cooled, 46, 90, 92
   pressurized-water, 44–45, 48, 89, 91, 92. *See also* Nuclear power plants
Nuclear Regulatory Commission (NRC), 51–55, 60, 68, 76, 77, 78, 81, 99
Nuclear Waste Policy Act (1982), 62
Nuclear weapons, 14, 69
   development, 15, 29–31
   fallout, 22, 31, 35
   production, 18
   proliferation, 20, 47, 89–90

Oak Ridge National Laboratory, 61
Oil, 93
Ontario Hydro, 67
Oppenheimer, J. Robert, 31

Philippines, 23
Photovoltaic cells, 97
Plasma, 83, 92–93
Plutonium, 20, 27, 28, 31, 33, 46, 48, 49, 60, 75, 89, 90
   effects on health, 46–47
   extraction, 48
   theft, 47
Pripet, Soviet Union, 84

Rabi, Isidor Isaac, 31

Rad (radiation absorbed dose), 35
Radiation
   effects of exposure to, 22, 31–33, 35, 36, 81, 84, 89
   exposure limits, 55
   ionizing, 31, 35
   lethal doses, 35
   therapy, 33
Radioactive decay, 27
Radioactivity, 18, 20, 22, 27, 28, 58
Radioisotopes, 27
Radionuclides, 32, 58
Radon gas, 33, 35
Rancho Seco, 23, 77
Reagan, Ronald, 50
Rem (roentgen equivalent man), 35
Richland, Washington, 67
Röntgen, Wilhelm, 28
Roosevelt, Franklin D., 29
Rutherford, Ernest, 26, 28

Sandia National Laboratory, 74
Scandinavia, 84
Scram, 43, 54, 77
Shippingport, Pennsylvania, 16
Shoreham, 23, 99
Solar energy, 94–98
South Korea, 23
Soviet Union, 16, 22, 23, 40, 74, 82, 93, 97
Spent fuel, 20, 33, 48, 59–61, 65, 89
Strassman, Fritz, 28
Strauss, Lewis, 16
Superphénix, 47
Susquehanna River, 81
Sweden, 16, 23, 88
Szilard, Leo, 29

Szymanski, Jerry S., 62–63

Teller, Edward, 31
Tennessee, 47, 61
Third World, 95
Thornburgh, Richard, 79
Three Mile Island (TMI), 21–22, 53, 76–82
Tokamak Fusion Test Reactor, 92
Trinity, 31

Union of Concerned Scientists, 91
United Nations (UN), 15, 94
    International Conference on the Peaceful Uses of Atomic Energy, 15
    Scientific Committee on the Effects of Atomic Radiation, 37
Uranium, 14, 19, 23, 27, 33, 39–44, 46, 48, 60, 64, 79–80
    enrichment, 23, 30, 48, 52, 57
    isotopes, 27, 40, 89
Uranium Mill Tailings Control Act, 65
Utility companies, 22, 51, 53, 87, 99

Waste, radioactive, 20, 22, 33, 35, 57–69
    disposal, 20, 37, 39, 48, 57, 61–64, 66, 69, 89, 92, 99
    high-level, 59–64, 61
    low-level, 65–69
    reduction, 67
    reprocessing, 20, 46, 48, 50, 57
    storage, 20, 23, 48, 50, 57, 59, 60, 61, 62, 82
        cost, 62
        long-term, 61–64, 67
        temporary, 60
Water table, 58
Watkins, James D., 22
Wave power, 95
Westinghouse Electric Corporation, 44, 91
West Valley, New York, 49
Wind farms, 96
Windscale (Sellafield), 50, 75
World War II, 14

X rays, 28, 34, 35

"Yellowcake," 40
Yucca Mountain, Nevada, 62

PICTURE CREDITS

American College of Nuclear Physicians: p. 56; AP/Wide World Photos: pp. 17, 18, 24, 66, 76, 79, 80, 86, 91, 97; Department of Energy: pp. 12, 38, 41, 49, 54, 59, 71, 94; © Bettya Lane: pp. 83, 88; National Archives: pp. 14, 63; Reuters/Bettmann Archive: p. 73; Original illustrations by Gary Tong: pp. 21, 26, 30, 34, 45

ABOUT THE AUTHOR

ANNE L. GALPERIN, a graduate of Northwestern University, is a freelance writer working in the areas of health, computers, and environmental science. She has served as an associate editor for Macmillan and as a writer for *Windy City Times*, a national gay/lesbian newspaper. She is currently working as a researcher for *Village Voice* political columnist James Ridgeway.

ABOUT THE EDITOR

RUSSELL E. TRAIN, currently chairman of the board of directors of the World Wildlife Fund and The Conservation Foundation, has had a long and distinguished career of government service under three presidents. In 1957 President Eisenhower appointed him a judge of the United States Tax Court. He served Lyndon Johnson on the National Water Commission. Under Richard Nixon he became under secretary of the Interior and, in 1970, first chairman of the Council on Environmental Quality. From 1973 to 1977 he served as administrator of the Environmental Protection Agency. Train is also a trustee or director of the African Wildlife Foundation; the Alliance to Save Energy; the American Conservation Association; Citizens for Ocean Law; Clean Sites, Inc.; the Elizabeth Haub Foundation; the King Mahendra Trust for Nature Conservation (Nepal); Resources for the Future; the Rockefeller Brothers Fund; the Scientists' Institute for Public Information; the World Resources Institute; and Union Carbide and Applied Energy Services, Inc. Train is a graduate of Princeton and Columbia Universities, a veteran of World War II, and currently resides in the District of Columbia.

333/.7924/GAL
Galperin, Anne.
Nuclear energy, nuclear wast
c1992. 32863363   27.95

MAL

SCARBOROUGH PUBLIC LIBRARY
3 9017 02446 5626

21 x 7/95 8/95
36 X 5/97 97/07   L

THE
SCARBOROUGH
PUBLIC LIBRARY
BOARD

FEB 17 1993